A WOMAN'S
RIGHT TO
PORNOGRAPHY

A Woman's
Right to
Pornography

Wendy McElroy

St. Martin's Press ✷ New York

*To John Dentinger
and his gleam of wicked fun*

Design by Junie Lee

Library of Congress Cataloging-in-Publication Data

McElroy, Wendy.
    XXX : a woman's right to pornography / Wendy
McElroy.
       p.   cm.
    ISBN 0-312-13626-9
    1. Pornography.   2. Sex oriented businesses. I. Title.
HQ471.M38   1995   95-20241
363.4'7—dc20   CIP

First Edition: September 1995

10 9 8 7 6 5 4 3 2 1

Contents

PREFACE

Pornography benefits women, both personally and politically.

After reading this, anti-pornography (or radical) feminists will consider me a heretic—fit only for burning. Or, to put it in more politically correct terms, I am a woman who is so psychologically damaged by patriarchy that I have fallen in love with my own oppression. My arguments will be dismissed.

In other words, if I enjoy pornography, it is not because I am a unique human being with different preferences. It is because I am psychologically ill.

Anti-pornography feminists try to silence any real discussion of pornography. Catharine MacKinnon, for example, flatly refuses to debate women on this subject. Feminists who disagree are treated as traitors. Their bottom line is: Individual women must not be allowed to question the sexual interests of women as a class.

Liberal feminists often argue *against* censorship rather than *for* pornography. Many of them view censorship as being far too dangerous a solution to the "problem" of graphic sex. They believe censorship could and would be used to stifle the voices of women. Nadine Strossen's book *Defending Pornography* eloquently argues this point. In response, radical feminists consider their liberal counterparts to be the "dupes of men," or "co-conspirators in gender oppression."

Yet many liberal feminists accept the basic anti-porn assumptions of radical feminism. For example, they generally accept the idea that pornography degrades women. This agreement does not seem to create common ground, however.

Why? Because anti-porn feminists will not tolerate any attempt to apply freedom of speech to pornography. In her book *Only Words,* MacKinnon goes so far as to deny that pornography consists of words and images, both of which would be protected by the First Amendment. She considers pornography—in and of itself—to be an *act* of sexual violence.

For years, anti-porn feminists effectively silenced dissent on pornography. Here and there, a renegade like Sallie Tisdale became so fed up with being ashamed of her own sexual responses that she would admit to enjoying adult films. When Tisdale explained in *Harper's* how pornography enriched her life, her admission caused a sensation. Tisdale's latest book bears the same title as her pioneering article, *Talk Dirty to Me.* It continues her celebration of sex.

A group of hardy feminists are now standing up to defend pornography . . . as harmless, as pleasurable, as fun. Some of these women have worked in the porn industry for decades. Candida Royalle, for example, has risen through the ranks of that industry to become one of its most powerful producers.

But something is missing from their defense of pornography. In fact, four things are missing:

1. A realistic picture of how the pornography industry works;
2. A full-scale attack on the fundamental assumptions of anti-porn feminists;

3. A forum from which the women who work in the day-to-day business of pornography can air their views; and

4. A sense of how pornography benefits women and is essential to the health of feminism.

This book fills the gap.

It argues from the perspective of a much-neglected tradition within the movement: individualist feminism. Since the nineteenth century, this rich tradition has argued for women's rights on the basis of self-ownership: that is, it is a woman's body, it is a woman's right. Individualist feminism consistently applies this principle to all issues affecting women, including sexual ones. Radical feminists argue that women all have the same collective interest, and only one sexually proper choice. Individualist feminists celebrate the diverse sexuality of individual women.

This book provides pornography with an ideology. It gives back to women what anti-porn feminism has taken away: the right to pursue their own sexuality without shame or apology, without guilt or censure.

Chapter One introduces the reader to the real world of pornography. Most of the accusations leveled at this industry are empirical. For example, the claim that women are coerced into performing in front of the camera. Since the only way to check out an empirical claim is to do research in the real world, I investigated the porn industry "up close." I talked directly to the men and women who *are* the industry.

In doing so, I adopted the strategy of dealing specifically with hard-corn porn—the XXX variety. If the women who made bondage videos were not mistreated, then the women involved in soft-core productions were not likely to be victims of violence either.

Chapter Two asks: What *is* pornography? How can pornography be defined? And, without such a definition, how can we pass laws—or even judgments—regarding this issue?

Chapter Three presents an historical perspective on pornography, and is divided into two sections. The first section provides insight into how anti-pornography legislation in the nineteenth century damaged the women's rights movement. This is especially true in the area of birth control. The second section examines the rise and fall of modern feminism. It argues that radical feminism is destroying the principle "A woman's body, a woman's choice." It is also killing the joy in women's sexuality.

Chapter Four assaults the ideology of anti-porn feminism. It strips away the rhetoric of rage and reveals their attack for what it is. It is not a quest for truth or justice, but an attempt to impose an ideology I call "sexual correctness."

Chapter Five provides an overview of both the anti-censorship and the pro-pornography arguments presented by liberal feminists.

Chapter Six is an all-out defense of pornography. It argues from a individualist feminist perspective and provides the intellectual underpinning for the book's opening statement: Pornography benefits women, both personally and politically.

Chapter Seven introduces some of the women who work in pornography: actresses, publishers, political activists, and producers. They paint a picture of what the industry is like, and how they feel about the stigma attached to their work. This chapter provides something anti-porn feminists attempt to suppress: a forum for women in pornography.

Chapter Eight suggests how the porn industry could be changed to provide greater respect and protection for the women who work in it. For those readers who want to pursue pornography—whether on a personal or political level—I have provided a brief indication of where to write or phone for more information.

Chapter Nine reports on a meeting of COYOTE, the only national sex workers' advocacy group, with a membership of women in the business.

The Appendix consists of a survey I conducted of sex workers. It presents a real-world profile, rather than a caricature, of these women.

THE NEW THREAT TO PORNOGRAPHY

Many people who work in pornography breathed a sigh of relief when George Bush lost the 1992 election. "At last!" they exclaimed, "the censorship-happy Moral Majority won't have the ear of those in power." But the administration of President Clinton poses a unique threat to freedom of speech.

Political correctness now censors the workplace to prevent sexual harassment. At universities, scholars can no longer discuss gender differences without being punished or denied tenure. The Federal Communications Commission imposes huge fines on erring sexual views, like those of Howard Stern. Television nervously censors cartoons for fear of Janet Reno's doing so. In short, freedom of speech is under attack by a liberal government.

Pornography requires a tolerant society, and ours is running short on tolerance. It does not matter whether the intolerance comes from the right or the left, from the moral majority or the politically correct. Both are a death knell for pornography.

The majority of people are not fully committed to either the right or the left. Nor to either censorship or absolute freedom of speech. People are too caught up in the daily struggle for survival to pour a lot of energy into ideology.

If intolerance is growing, it is not because most people share radical feminism's ideological objection to graphic sexual expression. It is because something about pornography frightens them. Anti-porn feminists feed on their fear.

The message of this book is: There's nothing to be afraid of. Pornography is part of a healthy free flow of information about sex. This is information our society badly needs. It is a freedom women need.

O n e

Pornography As an Industry

MY BACKGROUND ON PORNOGRAPHY

Like everyone else, I thought I knew what pornography was. I first glimpsed it as a child, from the magazines my older brother hid in his dresser drawer, under his socks. I was seven or eight and the excitement of doing something forbidden was far more thrilling than any of the images in the magazines.

By the time I was an adult, I had lost that sense of mischief and innocence. It was replaced by genuine sexual stirring, and a painful inner suspicion that something was wrong with my reactions. Something was wrong with *me*. My childhood—in a rural and conservative family—had instilled a vague belief that sex was unsavory. Surely my fascination with it must be unsavory as well.

I embraced feminism as a teenager, but the movement did not relieve my confusion about sex and pornography. At that time, the feminist movement was developing the cracks that have now broken into an open schism over sex. One faction of the movement joyfully celebrated the wide range of women's sexuality, from motherhood to lesbianism, from masturbation to oral sex. Another faction vociferously condemned certain choices. Marriage and the family were oppression, heterosexual sex was rape, and pornography was violence.

Ideologically speaking, the latter faction won out. It won so decisively that, during the eighties, few feminists were willing to stand up and defend the graphic depiction of sex. Women were not willing to expose themselves to the backlash of contempt that would follow a confession of enjoyment.

For over a decade, I have defended the right of women to consume pornography and to be involved in its production. In 1984, when the Los Angeles City Council first debated whether or not to pass an anti-pornography ordinance, I was one of two people —and the only woman—who stood up and went on record against the measure. I argued that the right to work in pornography was a direct extension of the principle "A woman's body, a woman's right."

My defense was purely ideological. I knew little about the realities of the industry or about the women I was defending.

Over the last decade, the anti-porn voices in feminism have grown louder and more shrill. An assortment of accusations are routinely hurled at the porn industry. Perhaps the most common charges are that women involved in porn are coerced into performing; porn videos are actually documentaries of rape and torture; and pornography inspires men to rape women.

But the business of pornography exists quite apart from any ideological attack or defense of it. It is a fact, not a theory. As I read and reread the onslaught against pornography, I realized I knew next to nothing about the industry. It was time to do some field work. It was time to check out whether radical feminism's accusations were accurate. And whether my position was naive.

Specifically, I wanted to know:

1. Were the women coerced into performing pornographic acts?
2. How were the women treated otherwise?

3. How did pornography—as a business—operate?
4. What did pornography—as a lifestyle—look like?

The only way to have these questions answered was to ask them. To ask them of the flesh-and-blood people who produce pornography: the actresses who are said to be coerced; the producers who are said to be the beating heart of white male oppression.

THE CONSUMER ELECTRONICS SHOW

The Winter '94 Consumer Electronics Show (CES) was scheduled for early January in Las Vegas. CES is huge. The total number of exhibitors at the show I attended was 1,056. Exhibits occupied more than one million square feet of space.

I was drawn to CES by the Adult Video Section, where most of the hard-core pornographers in America had booths advertising their wares. Soft-core producers, such as *Playboy,* would not be well represented. Their more respectable status allowed them to network and advertise elsewhere with ease. Moreover, the soft-core and hard-core industries tend to put distance between themselves, much as rich and poor cousins often do.

Pornography was once an important aspect of CES because it pioneered the popularity of videotape. In the early eighties, the few major studio releases that were available on videotape cost about eighty dollars. The more reasonably priced pornography attracted a huge audience of men and couples who had a taste for adult entertainment, especially within the comfort of their own homes.

Today, major studio releases run about twenty dollars and they quickly become available on videotape, for purchase or rental. Cable channels such as Playboy, Spice, and Adam and Eve offer high quality pornography that people can tape off TV for themselves. Pornography has lost its edge in both the video marketplace and at CES.

Accordingly, the Adult Video Section of CES was housed in the Sahara Hotel, far from the main convention center.

I had prepared for CES in two ways: emotionally and intellectually. As an intensely private person, I quickly resolved the emotional side. I was going to stay with the intellectual side.

I drew up two lists of questions: one for women, the other for men. The questions for women focused on whether they were coerced into "performing pornographic acts." If not, how were they treated? My questions included: Have you ever heard of women being threatened into performing in pornography? How much are you paid for a sex act or for a video? Do you negotiate your own contracts?

The questions for men focused on how pornography functions as a business, with particular emphasis on how women were treated. These questions included: How long does it take you to shoot a video? How many women work for you in a technical capacity, e.g., behind the camera?

I wondered how the women would react to my being a feminist. I wondered if the men would be dismissive. I was more than a little nervous about appearing ridiculous.

I began to make "guerrilla feminist preparations." I carefully chose a wardrobe of "feminist drag": Reeboks, blue jeans, and oversized sweaters . . . and an ultra-conservative dress for the AVN Awards ceremony. I decided to wear little makeup, less perfume, and no jewelry. When I looked in the mirror, I looked like I was going to give a lecture on sex rather than investigate the real thing.

DINING WITH PORNOGRAPHERS

My first dinner in Las Vegas was a headlong dive into the hard-core industry. My husband and I waited at the reception desk of the Bally Hotel to link up with John Stagliano, who is arguably the most successful XXX pornographer in America. His nickname is "Buttman" due to the specific XXX niche his videos, such as *Face Dance I* and *II*, fill. After a telephone interview, Stagliano had invited me to dine with him. Another pornographer, John Leslie, was included as well. I was told that Leslie was of the "old school."

I had never met Stagliano, but I made a point of watching several of the videos he'd produced. Since John had a tendency to appear in his own work, I thought I'd recognize him. I did. My first impression of the porn producer: youngish, amiable, streetwise, and a bit on the L.A. trendy side.

John Leslie (*Talk Dirty to Me*) was waiting for us in a nearby Italian restaurant. Although Leslie is well known as a porn actor, I hadn't seen any of his work. I would have recognized him immediately if I had. The man made an impression: immaculately attired in black, with pure white hair, a face of stone, and ice-gray eyes. Leslie looked more like a mafia don than a porn star. He stood in stark contrast to Stagliano's comparatively boyish enthusiasm.

While Stagliano answered the first of my questions—What makes something soft-core rather than hard-core?—Leslie ordered two bottles of wine, one white, one red. As a connoisseur, Leslie sent one bottle back for a replacement; the other he liked well enough to have the waiter soak off the label to take home for future reference.

At first, Stagliano and I chatted about what constituted fetish porn, while my husband and Leslie discussed the growing importance of Canada's Niagara peninsula as a wine-producing region. In short, everyone felt each other out. Then, in a neutral manner, I steered the conversation toward the possibility that women were coerced into pornography. I asked whether the violence in hard-core porn, like the sex, was real, rather than simulated.

The response was electric. Both producers vigorously insisted: *All* of the violence was simulated. In fact, there were strict restrictions on *which* acts could be simulated. Stagliano explained that the hard-core industry was regulated, not by law, but by the threat of law. In 1978, the police had made it clear they would prosecute any hard-core sex video that went past certain unofficial, but well-known, limits. These limits included: no more than three fingers in a vagina or anus (no fist fucking); and, no urination or defecation. Although mild images of violence were still tolerated, the slapping of breasts and faces was in a legal gray zone.

Those consumers who wanted hard-core pornography with more extreme images of violence could still find it—but only from expensive imported tapes. Expensive, because their importation was illegal.

As to coercion into pornography—the claim that women are forced to commit sex acts for the camera—Stagliano described how his company, Evil Angel, screened the women they hired as actresses. At casting calls, he and his partner Patrick asked the women which sex acts turned them on. From their answers, the two men knew the roles in which to cast the women. "Only if a woman enjoys what she's doing," Stagliano assured me, "can she give a convincing performance."

As an example, he recalled a shy woman who had come in on an open casting call earlier that week. Physically, she was what he considered perfect: young, a good hard body, a pretty face. But, after the first few questions, he'd decided not to use her. She didn't seem comfortable enough with sex to project real enjoyment to a camera. Then, Patrick asked her about bondage and she reportedly "came alive." The woman was hired for a bondage scene.

When I pressed on about the possibility of coercion, Stagliano readily admitted that the industry was huge. Some women were almost certainly abused or misused. "This happens in every business," he explained, "from Standard Oil to banking." The most common abuse came from producers who manipulated women into performing sex acts to which they have not agreed in advance. Usually, the manipulation was in the form of peer pressure. For example, the director might comment, "No one else objects," or "You're holding up production for everyone else."

Stagliano had heard of a producer who refused to pay a woman for past work unless she performed a sex act to which she objected. The woman knew it would be useless to sue, because courts do not have a track record of sympathy toward sex workers. This gave the producer a strong hold over her.

The conversation drifted on to whether or not there was such a thing as a snuff movie. This is a movie in which someone is actually killed in front of the camera during a sex/torture scene. (My question had political significance. In New York, over a decade ago, when a porn movie purported to be a snuff film, feminists had almost rioted outside the theater in which it played. This incident was the beginning of the "Take Back the Night" movement, under whose banner feminists still march through the streets of major cities to protest violence against women.)

Stagliano had no first-hand knowledge of snuff movies. But "a reliable source" had assured him that the movie that had caused such a sensation had been a scam. The producers had wanted to make more money. They thought a simulated killing, advertised as real, would make the ticket price skyrocket. They were right.

Stagliano interrupted Leslie's preoccupation with food to ask if *he* knew of any snuff films. The answer was no, but Leslie conceded the possibility of amateur snuff films. As he put it, "There are a lot of really sick sons-of-bitches out there." But no one "in the industry" would be stupid enough to put a murder on tape so that it could be used against them in criminal proceedings. In over thirty years in pornography, Leslie said he had never seen a snuff film, even though he had seen almost everything else, including what looked like real violence in Japanese videos.

As to the original film that caused such a furor, Leslie informed me that if I took the time to watch the video, I would see how the post-production editor had simply spliced new scenes into an old movie. The older movie was Mexican or South American, he couldn't remember. "It wasn't even good editing," he said, shrugging.

Next, I opened up the subject of contracts by asking how they were negotiated with actresses. Did the women usually sign whatever was put in front of them? Did they argue over fees or residuals? Did agents get involved?

A friendly dispute broke out at the table. Stagliano claimed he didn't sign contracts before shooting a video because he felt it might hinder the creative process. He didn't use scripts either. Instead, he relied on "concepts" which evolved during production. This meant his videos assumed a life of their own, in the style of cinema verité. He insisted that a contract which specified acts in advance could interfere with his method of production.

(I discovered later that Stagliano was one of the key producers who spanned pornography's transition from large-budget films to the currently booming amateur, or home, porn. During the seventies, porn films like *Behind the Green Door* and *Emmanuelle* had substantial budgets, trained actors, high technical values, and complex scripts with intricate plots. Today, the fastest growing sector of porn is home videos. These are videos which are shot by "regular" people—husbands and wives, boyfriends and girlfriends—who then sell them to distribution companies. The final tape combines several of these short amateur presentations under one label.)

Stagliano seems to fall between the two extremes of the seventies: big-budget and home porn. As a producer, he prides himself on technical values, especially on camera angles. The opening scene of *Face Dance I* still leaves me open-mouthed. But his videos do not have large budgets, prepared scripts, or the other trappings of the major productions of yesteryear.

As Stagliano explained why he didn't sign contracts in advance, I flashed on the anti-pornography ordinances which radical feminists had tried to push through various city councils a decade before. Under these ordinances, a woman who had performed a pornographic act could later bring a civil suit against the producer for "coercion into pornography." This would not have been a criminal charge. But it could have resulted in huge settlements for the woman. I wondered if Stagliano realized that his devil-may-care approach to contracts could have placed everything he owned in jeopardy.

Clearly, pornography had grown up as an underground industry. It had evolved by working outside the judiciary—outside the context of courts and contracts. The police and the legal system were still seen as hostile forces. And rightly so. If a contract was violated, it was touch-and-go whether a judge would even hear the case, let alone take it seriously. Women in porn were more likely to be mistreated by the police than protected by them. No wonder legal paperwork was given low priority.

"So far I haven't needed contracts." Stagliano seemed puzzled by my concern.

"What if you end up in court?" I asked. "If you don't have an enforceable contract, what are you going to do?"

"Why would I go after these people, Wendy?" he replied with a disapproving frown. "They don't have anything." He obviously thought I was heartless.

Before I could explain that these people might go after *him*, Leslie interjected, "I always sign contracts and releases in advance, just to get rid of the paperwork." Apparently, he was exhausted by the end of a project and didn't like to spend time at that point on loose ends.

The discussion of contracts quickly devolved into a heated denunciation of what Leslie called the "studio system." This is a system by which certain companies place aspiring porn actresses under exclusive contract. Typically, the contract promises the woman $5,000 to $10,000 a month. In exchange, the actress agrees to appear in some defined number of movies each month over a period of time, usually running from six months to a year.

Both Stagliano and Leslie loudly lamented this system. Why? Because it attracted the best looking and most talented women. This kept the actresses out of the "job market"—that is, out of *their* videos. To add insult to injury, the offending companies invariably produce "tame" material—an artistic choice that elicited scorn from the table.

(By "tame," they did not necessarily mean soft-core. Companies like Vivid Video *do* produce hard-core movies. But they are so sensitive to implications of violence against women that they shy away from even the suggestion of dominance, for example. Moreover, Vivid's hard-core videos are routinely edited down to soft-core versions for sale to adult cable channels.)

To me, the studio system made sense. It provided real benefits to the women who signed on. Not the least of these benefits was a decent, steady income over a predictable period of time. This allowed the women to make plans—to go back to school, for example.

Later I learned that a porn actress on her own earned only $150 to $600 for a day's work. I became even more impressed by the studio system. After all, most of the women who signed those contracts had limited education and limited job opportunities. And the fact that the movies were "tame" meant the women had a better chance of moving from porn into "legitimate" film. No wonder the studio system attracted women with talent and beauty.

I refrained from making such comments, however. My perspective was clearly out of step with the rest of the table.

I did continue to steer the conversation on to the broad subject of women in the industry. Did they like their work? Did they enjoy the sex scenes?

I asked the two producers what percentage of female orgasms in videos did they think were real. Both men immediately volunteered that one hundred percent of women's orgasms in soft-core videos were faked. But they disagreed radically about orgasms in hard-core porn. Leslie claimed that ninety percent of them were real. And that he could always tell. Stagliano estimated that ten to twenty percent of the women's orgasms were real. But he added, "The important thing is not the orgasm, but whether the woman shows real pleasure." He thought most women got involved in pornography to indulge a strain of exhibitionism within themselves.

I asked if the actors were also into "exhibitionism," or did they get something fundamentally different out of performing for the camera? Two comments shot straight back: Men get less money than women do, so money was less of a motivation; and, male orgasms are always real.

Do you think men and women enjoy different types of pornography? I asked, and the table fell silent. My husband came to the rescue by mentioning a magazine article that claimed women prefer "softer" movies, with more plot development, romance, and foreplay. Stagliano thought there might be something to this theory. His tentative agreement was overruled by Leslie's insistence that men and women reacted in *exactly* the same manner. As proof, he elaborated on how orgasms have the same effect on both sexes: an intensity in the eyes, flared nostrils, heavy breathing.

At this point, the pasta had been eaten; the wine had been drained; it was time for dessert. Conversation drifted away from my priorities and onto Leslie's extremely graphic reminiscence of a Scandinavian girlfriend. I remembered the words with which Stagliano had ushered me into the restaurant only an hour before:

"Now you'll get a candid look at the psychology of pornographers."

I also remembered my husband's comment on Howard Stern's book *Private Parts*, over which I had been laughing the night before. "This is how guys talk about women when they are just hanging out together," he had assured me. As Leslie warmed to his topic, I put my notebook away and began to eavesdrop.

At some point, I must have turned beet-red, because Stagliano leaned over and whispered, "Don't be embarrassed." Before coming to CES, I had resolved not to be prudish. For one thing, my background was hardly that of a wallflower. For another thing, I knew that sexual morality was largely a matter of geography and of the subculture you happen to be moving in.

Nevertheless . . . I *was* embarrassed, but not by the explicit language, or by what anti-porn feminists would call "reducing women to sexual parts." I was embarrassed by the loudness with which Leslie described "a fuck in the alley." At every table within listening distance—and that included a fair number—people were gawking at us. Conversation in our end of the restaurant had ceased, except for the pointed jokes and comments being muttered back and forth, all aimed at our table. Two women made their disapproval clear through glares and scowls directed, oddly enough, at me! I was thankful there were no children within earshot. At Leslie's description of "jerking off" to a phone call, another few tables fell silent.

As the blood pounded in my cheeks, I did what usually helps bring things into focus: I switched into critical mode. I analyzed the situation. I reached my first conclusion about the psychology of pornographers. They do not consider sex to be a private matter. This may seem to be a facile and painfully obvious insight. But—until then—I had thought pornography might be a business that shut down at five o'clock, like a post office.

This conclusion was confirmed as the convention progressed. People in the industry kept telling me intimate and unsolicited details about their sex lives. I realized that pornography was as much an attitude or lifestyle as it was a business. The line between private and public was sometimes blurred to the point of being erased.

The attitude toward sex in porn circles was like a brass band, with red tasseled uniforms, blasting its way down Main Street. The attitude was: Sex should be flaunted; conventions are to be scorned; shocking people is part of the fun; and, we are the sexual sophisticates, we are the sexual elite.

Yet, mixed up with this in-your-face approach was a strange eagerness to be understood and to be taken seriously by the regular world. Several times in the middle of a conversation, I suddenly realized it was important to the people I was talking to that I accept them, that I like them.

As Leslie talked, I reached a second conclusion. The porn industry reminded me of the gay community, in which I am lucky enough to have a few good friends. Before I'd been adopted as a "sympathetic" outsider, I had encountered a strange blend of suspicious hostility and total openness. This mix was sometimes manifested in the same person within the same ten-minute conversation. People in porn reacted to me in a similar manner. And probably for a similar reason. They were used to being rejected, even despised, by the people around them. On one level, they hungered for decent treatment and acceptance from the "legitimate" world. On the other hand, they had acquired the survival skill of automatically treating others with the contempt they fully expected to receive back.

These were the raw theories spinning out in my head when the only truly offensive comment of the evening occurred. As Leslie finished the account of the Scandinavian encounter, he made a casual remark that went right through me.

"She was gorgeous—totally fucked-up psychologically, but, oh, what an ass!" he exclaimed. Perhaps I overreacted. Perhaps I was more embarrassed than I realized, but it bothered me to hear a woman's angst being dismissed so lightly, while the curve of her ass was eulogized. I wondered if some of the criticism leveled at pornographers was accurate: Perhaps they did treat women like commodities—to be valued, but never respected.

After dinner, we retired to a music-blaring, smoky bar, which spelled death for conversation. Miraculously, there was an empty chair next to Stagliano's business partner, Patrick Collins. In their company Elegant Angel/Evil Angel, Patrick constituted the "Elegant Angel" half.

Conversation dissolved into screaming sentences at each other. From the snippets I caught, I gathered that Patrick and his wife worked as a team in the industry; she was nicknamed "Buttwoman." He had abandoned an upscale career in investment banking in order to pursue "excellence" in the one area that gave him satisfaction: graphic sex. Collins, with his gentlemanly way of speaking, was an antidote to Leslie. But the screaming was rough on my throat and I finally settled back to watch the crowd.

A young blond woman, with a hard face and an equally hard body, came over and ran her fingers persistently through Stagliano's hair. He had barely acknowledged this, when a brunette in incredibly tight jeans sat down in his lap and began to grind her hips into his groin. From my days of working in television, I'd seen this sort of behavior—in a more subtle form—displayed by women toward TV producers whose favors they wished to garner. It surprised me to see it displayed toward a porn producer. Perhaps I had accepted, on some level, that women *were* seduced and coerced into the industry.

Another theory began to spin out. What if pornography were nothing more than a dark mirror of the movie industry? A more blatant version of everything that goes on in Hollywood? What if the same basic rules of supply and demand, power and persuasion, mirrors and smoke apply to *all* producers and actresses, legitimate or not?

Having spun out this speculation, I began to punch holes in it. One immediate difference came to mind: There were no unions in porn, no SAG, no AFTRA, no ACTRA. Without their presence, pornography did not mirror—even darkly—any other aspect of the entertainment industry.

There was no protection from courts, which routinely dismiss suits brought by pornographers against distributors as "frivolous." Nor from police, who are far more likely to harass than to protect sex workers. This, too, was a difference of kind, not degree.

There was no genuine respect for hard-core pornography, except on the shadowy fringes of society. No mainstream newspapers, magazines, or TV news shows would review porn movies. No talk shows would invite the women as guests, except as curiosities. The better the women were at their trade—the expression of sex—the less likely they were to receive respect.

Too tired to speculate further, I walked away from the bar and the unfolding party scene.

THROUGH THE LOOKING GLASS DARKLY:
A DAY WITH THE INDUSTRY

By eight in the morning, most of the regular exhibitors at CES were running at full throttle, demonstrating their products to anyone who wandered by. I had been warned that the Adult Section operated on a different timetable. It would not start buzzing until after noon, perhaps because of the parties that tended to run into dawn. I decided to check out the larger convention and get a better context for the Adult Section.

The size of CES was stunning. A sea of booths hawked the latest in automotive technology, the best in audio and visual systems, the most sophisticated burglar alarms, and much more. The fastest, the biggest, the loudest, the best. And, in many booths, well-endowed women in revealing outfits leaned forward to smile brightly at interested passers-by, almost all of whom were men.

With a better sense of CES, I caught the shuttle back to the Adult Section, which was located a safe mile or so away from the more respectable exhibitors. Even within the distant Sahara Hotel, the Adult was isolated. An escalator provided the only access. At the bottom, two security guards checked badges to make sure those who entered were at least twenty-one years old. At the front doors of the exhibit hall, two more guards gave people a similar once-over.

It was nine o'clock and the Adult Section was stone-quiet; most booths were unoccupied; most aisles were empty. I wandered around, looking at the displays. Some fifty exhibits offered a broad spectrum of sexual material and information. The offerings ranged from fetish videos to phone sex services to a Free Speech counter. At the latter you could leave a donation in a gold fish bowl sporting a sticker declaring "Stop Censorship!"

I picked up literature and took notes on posters advertising XXX movies. Over and over again, I was struck by how attractive the women were: young, aerobically lean, and overwhelmingly blond. From over their shoulders, bent over peering through the V of their legs, sprawled on beds, looking up from on their knees—they all stared back at me with attitudes that ranged from submission to brazen bitchiness.

On my second tour of the floor, I approached the few people who were available and introduced myself as a feminist doing research on pornography. (After three such introductions, I dropped the word "feminist" because it seemed to alienate people.) Since no women were evident, I tried to get a sense of the "business of porn" from the men.

They were all in a mood to complain. Apparently CES had circulated a memo that morning to the Adult exhibitors, laying down strict rules of conduct. The rules included no full frontal nudity and no display of private parts. A burly red-bearded man, who was demonstrating interactive computer pornography, took particular exception to the abrasive security guards who ensured that photos of women's nipples and vaginas were duly covered by black dots. The hotel management had provided sheets and sheets of these dots.

When I asked security for a copy of the memo, they were strangely unable to find one. Two days later, I got a copy of the memo from Bill Margold, a veteran of the porn industry, who goes by the moniker "Bear." In the meantime, I had received three competing theories from exhibitors about sheets of nipple-concealing dots:

• They resulted from an incident of the year before. A buxom actress had gotten carried away with enthusiasm at meeting fans and impulsively bared what have been called "the best two things about her videos."

• They were a backlash against another incident from the year before. An after-hours fund-raising tent had been pitched in one of the hotel parking lots. Entertainment had been provided by several women, who engaged in a public sex act. The City of Las Vegas had laid charges, which included "felony sodomy" and "felony lesbianism."

• Nothing had changed. The rules were exactly as they had always been.

As exhibitors rushed to contradict each other, I began to realize that the porn industry was not a monolith.

As many of them shrugged off the incident, I realized something else: Pornographers were inured to being treated with contempt. What other industry would so blithely accept not being able to display its wares at its own conference? How many other exhibitors at CES would tolerate the intrusive surveillance of security guards, who constantly toured the floor?

MY FIRST INTERVIEW WITH A WOMAN IN PORN

A session of the Free Speech Coalition—an organization that protected porn producers and distributors from prosecution—was scheduled at noon. I arrived early to find three people present: Bill Margold; a man engaged in vigorous conversation with

Bill; and, Cookie—a thin blond who looked like a little girl. I overhead the man asking Bill whether things had been arranged with Cookie. Apparently, he wanted her to appear in a video he was producing. Bill shrugged and replied, "She's over there. Ask her yourself."

I'd heard Bill was an agent, so I opened a conversation by asking how people usually got into "the business." He referred vaguely to casting calls; then he said something surprising.

"I discourage people from getting into porn," he explained, "because you have to have a death wish to succeed at it." He expanded on this theme. "Pornography gets into your blood and you can never get away from it. No matter how many hard knocks you take, you'll always be part of the industry."

Since I'd met people who *had* left the business, I doubted the truth of this. But Stagliano had made a similar point, when he had enthused about the people in porn being society's "last outlaws, the last renegades." He had explained that being a stripper or a porn actress set you apart from respectable people. You became a social untouchable. Anyone who willingly accepted this stigma did so because they loved what they were doing. There was something inside of them that *had* to come out.

The grain of truth in this was worth puzzling over. I would do almost anything to be a writer, which involves nothing so much as an ostentatious display of my mind and opinions. What if other women felt the same way about displaying themselves sexually? I always prefer to be published by magazines with wide circulations. Why wouldn't they want to be seen by as many people as possible? Was there that much difference in the two forms of exhibitionism?

When Cookie drifted out the door with a clipboard in her hand, I followed. As a veteran of political meetings, I figured she had pulled hostess duty. That is, she was the pretty face delegated to greet people at the door and make sure they signed the mailing list.

I resolved to conduct my first interview with a "woman in the industry." Things began well enough. I asked Cookie if she had time for a few questions. She said yes and gave an insecure little-girl laugh, which seemed to punctuate all of her sentences.

I asked whether or not she signed contracts with the producers for whom she worked. She looked confused. I explained that there seemed to be no standard in the industry as to whether or when contracts were required. I was curious about what her experiences had been. Cookie laughed, then frowned, then said she only worked on videos. It wasn't like she was making movies or anything.

When several men came up to inquire about the upcoming meeting, Cookie seemed relieved to escape my scrutiny. One of the men had "Peterborough, Ontario" on his name badge. I identified myself as a fellow Canadian and we chatted about the adult video store he was planning to open up North as his retirement business. I asked if he would be affected by the 1992 Canadian Supreme Court ruling, called the Butler decision, which restricted the importation of pornography on the basis of the psychological damage it might do to women. He said he wasn't concerned since he didn't carry material that portrayed violence or exploited children. "And that's what people are really going after!" He went on to rail against violence on television and in mainstream movies.

Sitting there, I began to glimpse a political line in the sand that industry people were drawing. On one side was sex, which was good. On the other side was violence, which was bad. Yet it was the rejection of violence (primarily against women) that was driving the anti-porn crusade.

An alleged cause-and-effect link between pornography and violence against women had been the theme of the barely aborted Pornography Victims' Compensation Act (S.1521) of 1992. This act would have devastated pornography in America. It would have permitted crime victims to sue the producer, distributor, exhibitor, and retailer of any book, magazine, movie, or music that victims claimed had triggered the crime. There was no limit to the damages a victim could claim.

In other words, a woman who claimed her rapist had been inspired by a centerfold could sue *Playboy* for "causing" her assault. The organization Feminists for Free Expression (FFE), founded in 1992 to fight censorship, was instrumental in defeating this Act. FFE pinpointed the intellectual sleight-of-hand that occurs whenever violent crimes are blamed on words or images, rather than on the criminals who commit them. As FEE commented:

"Violence against women and children flourished for thousands of years before the printing press and motion picture. . . . Correlation studies, in this country, Europe, and Asia, find *no* rise in sexual violence with the availability of sexual material. No reputable research shows a causal link between 'obscenity' . . . and violence."[1]

The Peterborough storeowner was one among many industry people who seemed eager to concede that violence on TV leads to violence in the street. Yet, in agreeing that images and words are threats to safety, he virtually conceded the entire anti-pornography position.

Finally, Cookie was free again. I resumed the interview, which I now realize must have resembled an inquisition. I asked if she had ever been "coerced into performing a pornographic act." The question had one salutary affect: She stopped laughing nervously. She scowled out the word no. I asked if she knew of anyone who had been coerced. At this point the scowl deepened into genuine annoyance. She repeated no and looked pointedly away.

I closed my notebook, put aside my pen, and apologized for not having better questions to ask. My apology was strategic. Bill Margold had urged her to talk with me and I knew Cookie was insecure enough to blame any unpleasantness on herself. I didn't want her to feel she was to blame.

In fact, my questions were precisely the ones I needed to have answered. It was my technique that needed work. I had treated Cookie like a case study, instead of a human being. She was not a lab animal—she deserved courtesy. Thereafter, I asked women about violence only when the conversation provided a natural segue.

SWITCHING METHODOLOGY MIDSTREAM

The experience with Cookie made me rethink my methodology.

I decided to squelch the skepticism I had about what people were telling me. This was difficult, because I tend to doubt most of what I hear. With people in the industry, my skepticism was heightened by at least three factors:

1. Pornography is filled with people who are good at a con. This may have more to do with their being in entertainment than being in porn. Anyone who can raise money to produce a picture, or who can draw a performance out of an actor or actress, is *good* at manipulation.

2. I was new to the real world of pornography. Most of my information came from the sex-bashing rhetoric of radical feminism. I was beginning to realize how much of this was misinformation. This left me with no sense of perspective, no background against which to check the probable truth or falsehood of statements I was hearing.

3. I had a bias: I wanted women in the industry to be mentally competent adults. I didn't want to believe that they were like three-year-olds who should be stripped of the right to make choices. I was entering the situation with a prejudice. This was not an insuperable barrier, but it definitely raised a red flag.

I began to critique my own methodology as though it were that of a stranger. The first thing I'd want to know about the researcher was his or her underlying assumptions. Mine have already been detailed.

Next, I would object to the anecdotal nature of the report; that is, it does not contain hard statistics or double-blind studies. Fortunately, my research was aimed at countering accusations against pornography, which are also anecdotal. For example, the allegation that women are coerced into pornography is based on first-person accounts, such as the one provided by Linda Lovelace. Perhaps the most appropriate response to such data is "in kind."

A third problem with my methodology was the sweeping statements I made based on a limited exposure to the industry. Was I generalizing from too few particulars? Fortunately, for my purposes, generalizations were not necessary.

The anti-porn claim is that *every* woman in porn has been coerced into the industry, either through direct violence or indoctrination. All I had to do was to discover *one* woman who had not been so coerced. This would disprove the accusation. (This follows the old logic-book example: All that is necessary to disprove the assertion "All swans are white" is to find one black swan.)

In the final analysis, I settled for offering an honest account of my impressions of the industry. Short of laboratory conditions, no one could do more.

THE UNDERLYING POLITICS OF PORN

As I returned to the room, the meeting commenced with a dramatic flair. Bill Stolbach (nicknamed "Pinkie"), the president and founder of the Free Speech Coalition, had suffered a heart attack the day before and was still in a Las Vegas hospital.

A woman named Carol read the speech Pinkie had prepared before his heart attack. It began by stating the original purpose of the organization: to help all manufacturers, distributors, and storeowners combat the problems they had with the justice department: "to stop the cancer of censorship that is killing the industry" by providing an organization in which everyone stood firm together. Unfortunately, Pinkie noted, industry politics were destroying the Free Speech Coalition.

In his words, " . . . only a few give a shit as to what happens to others. In this industry, it seems that people are only out for themselves. . . . We have had people go to jail, people who are now facing jail sentences and big fines for no reason at all. . . . There are so many of you out there who would not join the organization because someone on the Board would not give you special pricing or some other stupid reason. . . . Does anyone here think that because you have an organization the government will just roll over and give up?"

In conclusion and in frustration, Pinkie resigned as president of the Free Speech Coalition. His speech closed: "I hope to God that no one else in our industry will have to go to jail. God bless all of you who have supported us."

An uncomfortable silence hung over the room. Without commenting on the resignation, a series of speakers presented their analysis of the "political state of porn." I was familiar with one of them, attorney David Wasserman, because of his writing on freedom of speech. Wasserman began by declaring that although the Clintons were in power, the battle wasn't over; it had only changed. I found this encouraging, until Wasserman called on the audience to support "our President."

This was the same President who had appointed Janet Reno—the woman who'd threatened television producers with stiff regulations if they did not squelch violent images, like those contained in Bugs Bunny. Her reasoning: People imitate what they see on TV. (Ironically, this is the same point Dan Quayle made when he suggested that shows like Murphy Brown were partially responsible for the increase in illegitimate children. Media people went crazy over Quayle's comment. They screamed out that Murphy Brown was a fictional character. But when Reno took a similar stand, there was silence.)

Industry people seem to be lulled by Clinton's imagined sexual tolerance. The result?

John Weston stood at the podium and declared, "Look at this. Nobody's here. In recent years, this room has been the hardest ticket to get into . . . two-thirds of the seats are empty. Where is everybody?"

Fewer than one hundred people were present. In a *Newsweek* article (January 1994), Catharine MacKinnon had informed readers, "Pornographers are worried. . . . They do sit around in rooms and figure out how to try and discredit what we're doing and destroy our credibility." (Obviously, this planning session was one I did not attend. More's the pity!)

The meeting dissolved into Q&A.

The most interesting audience comment came from a video store owner from New York City. He had attended a task force meeting called by the Mayor of New York, who wanted to ascertain if the sex industry should be regulated. The storeowner said that everyone who got up spoke "so bad [sic] about people in the industry" he felt embarrassed to be there. When his turn came, he told the task force that he was a resident of the city, a parent who paid his taxes and swept the sidewalk in front of his store. He told them, "You may not like my product, but I have a right to be there."

After he'd finished speaking at the task force, a female sex worker had risen to say, "I am a parent as well and taxpayer and a past president of the PTA in Greenwich Village." *The New York Times* picked up the story. The storeowner said he had learned something from the task force meeting: It was important for people in the industry to be good neighbors who "got along." They should stop being on the defensive, and start standing up for themselves as a legitimate business.

MEETING THE WOMEN OF PORNOGRAPHY

It was after 2:30.

The Adult Section was a buzzing hive of activity. The aisles were crowded. Behind booths, women in peek-a-boo gowns and skimpy costumes assumed poses for the fans; they signed photos and handed out membership forms for their fan clubs. I encouraged my husband to stand in line after line for autographs so I could stand beside him and observe the women give him the "fan" treatment.

Some lines were quite long. The pleasanter the woman was, the longer the line, since she chatted and accommodated requests for photographs. One petite brunette had about thirty men (and me) waiting: I found myself standing behind an impatient fan in a T-shirt that read "Will work for sex." When he reached the front of the line, the brunette scanned his chest and asked with admirable innocence, "Do you lay tile?"

In booth after booth, I watched how the women handled themselves. Some looked tired; some were obviously playing a role; others seemed—as one woman phrased it—"high on life." But at least two things were constant:

All of the women treated fans well. I remember one blonde in a tight and sequined emerald-green gown that made her look like a mermaid. She was posing with a shy Asian man who'd requested a photograph. Handing the camera to a friend, he placed a tentative right arm around her waist, letting the left arm dangle at his side. She reached over and placed his left hand on her hip. The man beamed. Off to the side, a burly bouncer watched the interaction closely, ready to step in at any sign of the woman's being mistreated.

All of the women seemed to have fan clubs, which cost money to join. Membership costs ranged from a one-time fee of about twenty-five dollars to a similar yearly sum. The fee seemed to depend on what the clubs offered for the money. All of them advertised "personal" responses to letters. All of them entitled members to "very special gifts," "truly daring photos," and "items never made available to the general public." The ones with yearly fees seemed to have the added incentive of monthly newsletters.

My favorite club featured the blond and buxom Kitty Foxx, who promoted "XXX-Rated Videos of Mature Women in Hardcore Action." True to the ad copy, Kitty was a fetching older woman with the rounder curves that come with maturity. The videos she hawked were entitled *Older, Bolder and Better* Volumes One and Two, both of which had been produced by her own company. After talking with her, I got a photo picture inscribed "Love your attitude! Kitty."

Next, I stopped at a booth that sold *Hot Spots*—a guide to hot night clubs and novelty shops. The co-author, "Jane" (aka porn queen Veronica Hart), was signing autographs and greeting fans. When I reached the head of the line, I went into my patter. "Hi, I'm a writer who's covering the Adult Video Section of CES, and I wanted to see how things are going for you." Somewhere, the word *feminist* arose, because "Jane" erupted:

"I don't need Andrea Dworkin to tell me what to think or how to behave." She seemed genuinely angry. "And I don't appreciate being called psychologically damaged! I have friends in the business who call themselves 'Anarchists in High Heels.' They'd love to have a word with her."

I must have looked stunned, because she abruptly stopped talking. She was the only woman at the convention to bring up radical feminism, and it threw me so totally off guard that I still don't remember how I responded. At the words "Anarchists in High Heels," I looked straight down at my Reeboks. "Jane" shook her fist in the air and declared, "Don't worry, we'll fight for your right to wear sneakers, too!" I suddenly felt outradicaled.

Another fan took advantage of my confused silence to catch

her attention. A perplexing emotion consumed me: I was depressed. My husband kept asking me, "Are you okay?" Finally, I admitted that the exchange had depressed me and I didn't know why. He burst out laughing.

He explained it to me. "Jane" was the first woman to challenge me on my own intellectual ground.

I had to admit: He was right. I felt threatened. I felt bested. I realized that my defense against being sexually intimidated by these women was a belief in my intellectual superiority. My trip to CES was the political equivalent of missionary work in deepest Africa, where I had found a native who spoke English with an Oxford accent. No wonder my husband was laughing at me.

It was a chastened feminist who returned to the exhibit floor. The first booth I visited was Crystals, a company that does the artwork on the box covers of about eighty percent of the porn videos in America. There, an older and hard-looking woman explained that she'd been around the business for a long time. She made a point of telling me she'd put four children through college with money made from the industry.

"This convention's far more tasteful than it used to be," she assured me. "Of course, it used to be four times as big as it is right now," she conceded. And exhibitors used to be able to sell their product from the floor, whereas now they could only take orders to be shipped later. In the olden days, some companies used to make up two sets of invoices: a real one and a bogus one that read "Free samples only." The customer showed the bogus invoice to guards at the door. The tax people shut this practice down.

When I asked whether she thought more repression of pornography was coming, she assured me, "Reagan and Bush and that Meese crowd are out on their asses. I'm not worried about Clinton. I mean he's a liberal and I think he's even for pornography, isn't he?"

Is he?

THE PHILOSOPHY AND PRACTICE OF PORN

The only male star I saw signing autographs was Randy West, a blond with a wall-to-wall chest and a Dudley DoRight chin. I didn't get his autograph, but I picked up an ad for his new movie (*Up & Cummers*). It included a paragraph on his formula for producing pornography:

"I find the best looking, hottest new babes with up and cumming star potential. . . . Find out what turns them on & who they would like to be with, put them together and let them go wild. Live, for real, no script, no acting, no fake orgasms."

Producers seemed fond of giving their philosophy of porn. In another handout—this one an ad for *Sodomania: Tales of Perversity* by Elegant Angel—Patrick Collins described his slant on pornography:

"Sodomania is dedicated to all of us who hate watching women fuck that don't like fucking! . . . But if you like girls who like getting fucked in the ass, girls who like to lick cum off their toes, and girls who just love to suck . . .—Then this is the tape for you!"

As I read these accounts of "real action" and "natural sex," I wondered if pornography was relegating itself to an amateur status. After all, art is not natural; it is the opposite of nature. The best scripts and acting are consciously conceived and painstakingly sculpted; they come from skill and hard work, not from spontaneity. Pornography seemed to be eagerly defining itself out of the artistic realm.

This was confirmed by the fact that home porn is the fastest growing aspect of the industry. Home porn is short videos produced by "real" people, with ordinary bodies, who then sell the tapes of their sexual encounters for public viewing. Several short subjects are spliced together, then marketed. These videos were fairly inexpensive—e.g., nine tapes for about one hundred dollars. One exhibitor insisted that the tapes he received from amateur producers were far more innovative than the mass-produced ones. Moreover, buyers knew the action was real. The home porn market included newsletters, computer bulletin boards for downloading "full-motion video clips," and an introduction service for amateur fans.

A booth to my left promoted sex toys; on my right, a woman reached into a huge goldfish bowl full of condoms and handed them out to passersby. (Coin-sized and wrapped in gold foil, they reminded me of the chocolates I used to love as a child.) Interactive computer displays flashed porn with low resolution and a low update rate—ten or fifteen frames a second. Another booth distributed mock samples of "Prepaid Private Issue Calling Cards." The purchaser of such a card simply dialed an 800 access number, gave his authorization code, and was able to dial a list of sex phone lines. No phone calls showed up on his home or company phone bill.

Next I stopped at the *Adult Video News (AVN)* booth to ask about a matter that perplexed me. *AVN* is the trade publication for video porn. In the table of contents of the January issue, an article entitled "I've Finished My Calls, So . . ." was listed on page 20. A subtext described the article: "Our esteemed publisher comments on some of the less esteemed people in the adult entertainment business." The idea of the industry regulating itself by exposing malfeasance was interesting. But page 20 consisted of an advertisement. No article with that title appeared elsewhere.

A man at the *AVN* booth told me that the article had been yanked so quickly there had been no time to change the table of contents. Further inquiry resulted in a brush-off. I asked people at other booths to speculate about the matter. According to the best informed source, the article was about a porn producer known for writing rubber checks. It was disappointing that the magazine was unwilling or unable to expose fraud.

THE STICKY ISSUE OF SADO-MASOCHISM

The most prominent type of pornography at the convention seemed to be fetish porn, especially S/M and dominance. In one booth, women role-played at dominance and submission, using soft whips and other equipment. As I watched, I started to get upset—not because I thought the women were coerced or psychologically damaged, but because I don't like even "mock" humiliation.

And I was bothered by the reaction of the men. At one point, a producer from a public access station asked one of the women to "perform" so he could film her. She crouched down on her knees, her ass jutting into the air. With the hand farthest from the camera, she raised a whip and flicked it down across her backside, all the while moaning to herself to "do it harder." The producer kept shifting his position to get a better angle, or, maybe, just a better look.

This is my clearest memory of the convention and it never fails to disturb me. I am convinced that the woman performed of her own free will and that she was not physically harmed. She appeared to be enjoying herself. I am also convinced that my sexual preferences and reactions are no more natural than anyone else's. Nevertheless, a sinking feeling always accompanies this vivid memory.

In sorting through S/M videos and publications, I tried to answer three questions:

1. *Did the action looked staged?*
Invariably, it did. A few magazines showed photos of bruised women, but the marks were clearly makeup, with only one bruise vaguely resembling the real thing. There was one exception: the spanking magazines—usually imported from Britain—showed asses that seemed sincerely red. More than anything, the S/M magazines seemed campy.

2. *Did the men tend to dominate the women, or vice versa?*

I saw about twice as many cases of women dominating men than the reverse. For example, one of Bizarre Video's June releases was *Mistresses at War,* with the subtext, "A slave is torn between two dueling mistresses. Where does his loyalty lie?"

3. *How far did the mock violence go?*

The violence was restrained and less graphic than can be seen in many studio releases. Common sights included: someone in chains or wearing a collar; hair-pulling; women with fearful expressions; women on their knees (often in front of other women); and spankings.

But the fetish market is much more than S/M. There was porn featuring fat people, feet with painted toenails, women with incredibly large breasts, and a *Cousin Bubba* magazine advertising "Country Corn Porn."

To tell the truth, as I perused the S/M and other fetish porn displayed, I was not disgusted or distressed. I thought most of it was rather silly.

THE AVN AWARDS: THE OSCARS OF PORN

The Adult Video News (AVN) Awards Show is where excellence in the industry is recognized through awards such as "Best Editing for a Film," "Best Actor, Video," and "Best All-Sex Feature." On January 8, it was the hottest ticket in Las Vegas.

The room held 125 tables, which seated ten people each. My table—number 102—boasted a perfect stereo view of the stage via two huge screens to my right and left. Music boomed loud enough to make the floor quake and conversation impractical. I shared the table with an angry looking woman in a black dress and sequined red jacket. To her right sat a bored looking man. They were an attractive couple in a non-porn fashion—meaning they didn't look either hard or glitzy or thrilled to be there. The woman had an air of slumming.

From their silence, it was clear I would have to initiate introductions. They turned out to be doing a documentary on the U.S. porn industry. Trying to keep up the conversation, I asked the woman what had surprised her the most about the convention. She answered, "Nothing. There's nothing surprising here. I'm used to working in Hollywood."

To break the ice, I volunteered, "The thing that surprised me the most was how conservative these people are." This piqued the man's interest, who leaned his elbows onto the table. I expanded, "They all believe that the government will protect them now that Clinton is in power."

Both nodded agreement. The man admitted to not being "up" on the current state of censorship in the U.S. He asked me for a thumbnail sketch. I obliged, then launched into a critique of the class structure of pornography, wondering aloud where the new blood was. "Where are the Young Turks?" I exclaimed. The lady remarked, "One of them is seated across from you. You should go and talk to him."

Later I realized my enthusiasm must have irritated her. As the Awards ceremony progressed, the contempt in which she held people in the industry became obvious.

The Young Turk was named Greg Steel. About twenty-five years old, in a rumpled suit topped off by a Brillo-mop of red hair, Greg's appearance was in sharp contrast to the trendy "I'm into my body" look of the crowd. He provided a natural opening for conversation.

"You are the only person I have seen," I smiled, "who is wearing an AIDS ribbon. In a sexually aware crowd like this, I expected to see them everywhere." He offered that a friend of his had recently died of the disease and added that he produced gay as well as straight videos. In fact, he was up for an award in a gay category.

I asked how the "younger generation" conducted business differently than the older one. I learned that contracts were signed in advance; at the actresses' discretion, the actors used condoms; the actresses were asked whom they wished to perform with; scripts were prepared in advance and distributed to the cast for rehearsal; the minimum fee for a day's work was six hundred dollars. I was amazed; he seemed to approach pornography as though it were a craft, a profession.

When I asked about politics, Greg gave one of the most intriguing and dismissive answers I received. "I don't concern myself with politics," he said. "It doesn't interest me." Then he added, "Censorship has nothing to do with politics. They don't want to close us down. This is a huge industry and they want a cut of it."

I started to contradict him—to point out that the Religious Right and anti-porn feminists were on a *moral* crusade. Closing him down was precisely what they wanted. I stopped short. There was as much truth in his perspective as there was in mine. Most politicians probably *were* happy to let pornography exist . . . as long as it paid for the privilege.

Another Young Turk named Shawn Ricks and his protégé actress, Sydney, joined us. A tall blond woman sat down. And . . .

. . . The Awards ceremony began. The incredibly square-chinned Randy West hosted the event and began by singing, "It shows a lot of class to take it in the ass." Or, at least, that was the gist of the lyrics. Unfortunately, whoever mixed the sound must have learned his craft at rock concerts, because the instruments overwhelmed the voices. But the screens provided a perfect view.

As the Awards progressed, I ignored the other people at the table and chatted with Greg. A specific event triggered this decision. The blonde and the documentarian had been trading bitchy remarks about the people onstage. Perhaps the insults were accurate, or perhaps the two women were catty cynics. Whichever—their attitude made me feel ridiculous for enjoying myself and for admiring the "in your face" attitude of the industry.

The turning point: A flustered young actress burst into tears at receiving an award. When the other women at the table hooted in derision, my back literally bristled. Why shouldn't the woman cry? This was *her* night to be proud of her work, to be touched by the tribute of her peers. Who knows what abuse she swallowed from the world about how she paid her bills? Listening to the insults fly, I felt as though the casual cruelty of the regular world was sitting across the table from me.

Anger had a salutary effect. If being sophisticated meant having contempt for other women, then fuck it! I had a second glass of wine and settled back to enjoy myself.

Not knowing the videos or people up for awards was a barrier to appreciating the event. Instead, I cued in to the flow of the show and to the education I was getting from Greg.

As to the flow: Part Two of the ceremony focused on the technical and gay awards. This section was remarkable for its brevity. In other sections, the presenter read off the nominees and the winner rushed onstage to accept. In Part Two, only the winners were announced and only the most important gay awards were handed out in person. Since gay porn constitutes a huge chunk of the industry, this short shrift was puzzling.

I was even more baffled when Chi Chi—perhaps the most famous gay sex performer—capped off the Awards Event with a dazzling production number. On a Caesar-like reclining throne, he/she was carried onto the stage by slave boys, who proceeded to join in the musical number, "Love Doll." The audience couldn't seem to applaud or cheer loudly enough. *What was this?* I wondered. *A schizophrenia about gays?*

My political sensibilities perked up at two other points. The first: An elegant man stood up to receive a major award and people at table 102 began to mutter. Greg explained that the fellow had worked for only six months last year because he'd had a sex scene with a woman who'd turned out to be HIV positive.

Health certificates had become standard practice in the industry; I now wondered if they were as easy to forge as documents proving age.

The second incident concerned another Young Turk. A black producer named Sean Michaels was passed by for an award. Sydney, the lady on Shawn Ricks's arm, commented wryly that it would be a long time before the AVN presented an award to a black person. The next day, people to whom I mentioned this remark took exception. But they admitted that black men were not common in porn; Asian men were unknown. And they couldn't remember a black man ever winning in any category.

After this, the mood at table 102 changed. Everyone who'd been nominated, or connected with a nomination, had been passed over. It dawned on me how much these people had wanted to win. Now Shawn Ricks began to tell me about his philosophy of pornography. He wanted to be on the cutting edge, to break the rules. As I would do with any other young rebel, I wished him luck.

A SLEEPY SUNDAY IN PORN

A bright Sunday morning—and the Adult Section was deadly quiet. Fortunately, the one gay booth—which shared space with a straight company—was occupied by a lean young man and a plumpish woman.

I walked up, and into an interesting situation. A rather plain girl was asking how she could get into porn. The plumpish woman behind the counter cut her off coldly, because (as she later explained to me) the aspiring actress was so unattractive that the only honest answer would have been "in your dreams."

I was surprised to see a woman so eager to get into the industry. The woman behind the booth assured me that it happened all the time.

I began to wonder whether the reason porn actresses are poorly paid was simple economics. If there is such a glut of "talent" that people will perform for free, this would depress wages for everyone. The same would be true in the legitimate film business, if it were not for unions, which prevent "volunteer" labor. This might also explain why porn actresses are so good-looking; producers can pick and choose.

To open conversation, I asked the fellow in the gay booth whether porn actors ever crossed over into legitimate film. He said no, but that the reverse often occurs. People give up on "legitimate" careers and get stuck in porn, where they are stigmatized. He turned and addressed an imagined critic standing to his left. "I'm sorry, not all of us can do Seinfeld. I'm sorry, I have rent to pay."

I commented on how the absence of AIDS ribbons surprised me. He replied that gays were not well received by straight pornographers, who were into being "macho sex machines." Then he explained how gay porn had pioneered condom use within the industry. Every gay shoot, he insisted, had a big bowl of condoms that the actors were required to use. Grimacing, he said that producers of regular porn didn't even want to hear about condoms because they claimed, "The audience doesn't want to see them."

(Every discussion I had with straight producers confirmed this. For example, when I suggested the possibility of using the condom in a sexy manner—perhaps having the woman put it on with her mouth as a prelude to oral sex—I was told brusquely "It's been done." No one was interested in the ethical issue, despite the fact that there had been recent AIDS scares and scandals.)

The fellow added that gay porn *had* changed the straight industry in at least one way: The men were better looking, simply because gay actors were so attractive. I offered an alternative theory: Namely, more couples and women are consuming porn and —whatever feminists said—women wanted sexier men.

Upon hearing the word "feminist," a long, annoyed monologue erupted. "There is *no* coercion on any porn shoot," he assured me. "Everyone on a set knows *exactly* what is going on and *that's* why they're there."

For the rest of the day, the exhibit remained quiet, with some booths not even opening. I said my good-byes to the people who'd been generous with their time.

While I thanked Bill Margold, he took the opportunity to introduce me to a cherubic man who had invented phone sex lines. He looked familiar. I asked if he had attended a certain political meeting. He choked out an amazed yes. We had met years ago, in another context. A mild-visaged soft-spoken businessman, he would have never crossed my mind as a "sex worker." An accountant, maybe.

CONCLUSION

Pornography frightens people. Women in the industry threaten women who are not.

This became clear to me when I eagerly discussed my experience at the CES with girlfriends. Their reactions varied widely, but they all agreed on one point: I was a fool to have taken my husband along.

Two assumptions lurk beneath this reaction. First, men cannot be trusted. Second, women in porn are predatory.

The first assumption is a pure insult to men and not within the purview of this book. The second assumption is also an insult, directed at women in pornography. But it is a part of what this book is about.

Women in porn do not appreciate how much they intimidate "regular" women, who usually put in long hours at tiresome jobs before rushing home to feed their kids—all the while trying to retain the fading blush of youth or enthusiasm.

Such women are intimidated by the images of porn on several levels:

First, the women in porn today are extremely attractive:

young, with large, unsagging breasts and aerobicized asses. They are a walking reproach to women who are trying to lose weight and to tighten up what gravity is loosening. There is no way to compete with the image of sexual perfection that porn projects. A lot of the scorn heaped on women in the industry undoubtedly springs from feelings of inadequacy and jealousy.

Second, the women in porn seem to be sexually available, uninhibited, and easily satisfied—none of which is true for the rest of womankind. Whether it is *actually* true of women in porn is irrelevant: This is the image projected. And, again, it is almost impossible to live up to. After going through a great deal of angst over sex, I know who I am sexually and I like that person. But—even now—I am not perpetually available or totally uninhibited. I can only imagine the deep resentment felt by women who have real problems with sex.

Third, the women in porn receive a great of sexual attention from men—most of whom are husbands or boyfriends. This is upsetting to their wives and girlfriends, whose emotional and sexual needs are often being neglected. They blame the men. They blame the porn actresses.

For their part, women within the industry are less tolerant and sexually open than they imagine themselves to be. As accepting as these women are of each other, they can be strangely intolerant of outsiders. Some of this probably comes from a natural suspicion of the "regular" world, which usually treats them with disrespect. But much of the intolerance comes from a sense of sexual elitism.

People in porn consider themselves to be more sexually sophisticated and more liberated than the average person. They evince contempt for those who live conservative lifestyles—e.g., the midwestern housewife with three children and a monogamous marriage. They call these choices "uninformed" or "unnatural." They claim that the little housewife simply "doesn't know what she is missing"; if she did, she'd be stripping for the camera.

If the housewife retorted, with absolute accuracy, "You have no idea what the rewards of *my* lifestyle are," she would be dismissed out-of-hand.

I tried to argue that no choice was "right" for every person. Sexuality is richer than that: It is a banquet of choices and possibilities, none of which we can afford to dismiss. Yet over and over, in both small and large ways, I saw the "wrong" sexual choices being dismissed or ridiculed. They were not condemned as right or wrong, good or evil. Instead, they were disdainfully brushed away as uninteresting, boring, or mundane. The effect was the same.

For example, when I brought up the sexiest movie I've ever seen—*Sex, Lies and Videotape*—the incredibly disparaging comments that came back ensured my silence. True, I wasn't called perverted, only boring. I was left to wonder which I preferred.

So . . . what of the two main questions with which I approached CES?

Were women coerced into performing pornographic acts?

I saw no evidence that women are forced into performing pornographic acts. I saw overwhelming evidence of informed consent. Although I heard rumors of women who had been pressured into performing sexual acts, no one I spoke to had experienced it themselves. Of course, this does not disprove the rumors.

How were women in the industry treated otherwise?

Not especially well. Indeed, a few pornographers seemed determined to live up to society's worst caricatures of them. They spoke of women in brutally cold and dehumanizing terms, which appalled me. Other pornographers, who probably believed they did treat women well, actually displayed considerable contempt for them. These were the men who refused to deal with women as equals in contracts and negotiation.

At this point, men in the industry will loudly object that they acknowledge women as the core of their business. Without women, they will proclaim, the industry would not exist. This is a form of acknowledgment, but not a form of respect. Women in the industry are like thoroughbred horses, without whom there could be no day at the races. The women are valued, they are cared for, they are protected—but I didn't see them respected.

For example, when men spoke of each other—whether to praise or to bury—it was about their work, their accomplishments or lack thereof. So-and-so was a genius, active in the Free Speech Coalition, or a bad agent. Women were always discussed in terms of their physical components. This one has a good ass, that one's lost too much weight or her breasts are sagging.

As in every other endeavor—in or outside of the business world—women in porn will probably get respect only after they get power.

Two

DEFINING PORNOGRAPHY

If you wish to converse with me, define your terms.
—Voltaire

There is no way to approach pornography without first struggling with the most fundamental question that anyone can ask: What is it?

For decades, the most common nondefinition of pornography was the one used by Supreme Court Justice Potter Stewart in his concurring opinion on *Jacobellis* v. *Ohio*[1]

"I shall not today attempt further to define [hard-core pornography] . . . ; and perhaps I could never succeed in intelligibly doing so. But I know it when I see it. . . ."

Why is it so important to define pornography?

If people were not trying to pass laws against pornography, a definition might not be so crucial. But when courts become involved, definitions become essential. Whoever controls the definition of pornography will determine which words and images the law will suppress. They will decide the framework of future debate over pornography. Definitions directly influence how people think about an issue and the attitude with which they approach it. There is no mystery as to why anti-pornography feminists have spent so much time and energy in trying to define their terms. It is a quick and effective way to control the debate.

The purpose of definitions is to sketch the legitimate boundaries within which a word can be used. The beauty of definitions lies in their ability to let people know what they are talking about. Their magic is the clarity of thought that can result from drawing distinctions. Definitions are like the focus on a camera lens, bringing the intellectual outlines of an issue into sharp relief.

ELIMINATING NONDEFINITIONS

One step toward defining anything is to determine what it is *not*.

A popular approach to the word *pornography* is an appeal to its ancient Greek roots. This approach should be discarded. The word *pornography* originally meant "writing about harlots or prostitutes." But its meaning has evolved over centuries of use through dozens of different cultures. Like the Greek word *gymnasium,* which originally meant "place of nakedness," the word *pornography* has lost its connection with the past.

Nevertheless, Andrea Dworkin, in *Pornography: Men Possessing Women*, takes this "historical" approach:

"Contemporary pornography strictly and literally conforms to the word's root meaning: the graphic depiction of vile whores, or in our language, sluts. . . . The word has not changed its meaning and the genre is not misnamed . . . the graphic depiction of the lowest whores."[2]

Even granting that it is possible to understand the contemporary use of a word by referring to ancient Greece, this definition is a vacuum waiting to be filled. For example, in today's social context, what is a "slut"—especially to a woman, such as Dworkin, who openly denounces monogamous heterosexuality?

D. H. Lawrence—the brilliant novelist who was destroyed by censorship—claimed that a purely semantic definition of pornography offered no useful information at all. "The word itself, we are told, means 'pertaining to the harlots'—the graph of the harlot. But nowadays, what is a harlot? . . . Why be so cut and dried? The law is a dreary thing, and its judgments have nothing to do with life. The same with the word *obscene*: nobody knows what it means. Suppose it were derived from *obscena*: that which might not be represented on the stage; how much further are you?"[3]

Dworkin's definition may not transmit useful information, but it does clearly show her hatred of pornography. By calling pornography "the graphic description of the *lowest* whores"—when the adjective "lowest" is not in the Greek translation—Dworkin tells us more about herself than about the word *pornography*.

Moreover, the spectacle of radical feminists leaning upon the support of etymological authority is a strange sight indeed. After all, they adamantly reject the science and history of Western civilization as manifestations of white male culture. They reject the chronicles of history, because they are not *her*story. They rail against the hard sciences, because they spring from white male methodology. The white male study of etymology, however, is legitimate—at least, when it suits their purposes.

Enlightenment is not likely to come from anti-pornography feminists, who view the world through the lens of ideology. Their rhetoric is the linguistic equivalent of thermonuclear war. Pornography is called "genocide"; Susan Brownmiller describes it as "the undiluted essence of anti-female propaganda"; Judith Bat-Ada compares Hugh Hefner to Hitler; Andrea Dworkin's book on pornography begins by claiming "Men love death . . . men especially love murder."

Such descriptions are normative, or biased. They embody the viewers' reactions, and their desire to condemn pornography.

It is important to understand why anti-pornography feminists spend so much time and energy trying to define pornography. Definitions not only control the debate, they can control what sexuality itself becomes. Radical feminists view sex as a social construct. That is, they do not believe the current expressions of sexuality are inherent in human biology; instead, they are products of culture. If women's sexuality is a blank sheet of paper, then defining it becomes tremendously important. Whoever controls the definition will determine the content. The struggle to define pornography is part of radical feminism's attempt to control sexuality itself.

The stakes are high. High enough for freedom of speech to be jettisoned. Indeed, in her recent book *Only Words*, Catharine MacKinnon argues that pornography has no connection with free speech whatsoever; it is an *act* of sexual subordination, of sexual terrorism.

"Empirically, of all two dimensional forms of sex, it is only pornography, not its ideas as such, that gives men erections that support aggression against women in particular."[4]

Over the last decade or so, the feminist position on pornography has shifted toward this definition. Pornography is no longer viewed as merely offensive; it is redefined as an *act* of violence, in and of itself. It is the sexual subordination of women, by which their victimization is eroticized and perpetuated. It is the main way patriarchy subordinates women.

Other feminists have pointed out that rape existed long before *Playboy* appeared in the racks of corner stores. Such voices of reason are lost in the wind of hysteria. Anti-pornography feminists acknowledge them only to launch an *ad hominem* attack.

For better or worse, it is necessary to treat anti-pornography feminists with more respect than they are willing to give back. It is important to consider the substance of their definitions.

The anti-pornography definitions abound with emotionally charged and highly subjective terms like "humiliation" or "subordination." And they are commonly offered as the crowning statement of horrifying stories of sexual abuse.

Consider the opening of *Only Words*: "You grow up with your father holding you down and covering your mouth so another man can make a horrible searing pain between your legs.

When you are older, your husband ties you to the bed and drips hot wax on your nipples . . . and makes you smile through it."[5] Ms. MacKinnon springboards from this scenario into a discussion and definition of porn.

In January/February 1994, *Ms.* magazine featured the issue of pornography. In an open discussion between a group of feminists, the following definitions were offered:

> Pornography is the use of sex to intimidate and/or control women and children. . . . It has to do with depicting something that is violent and possibly life-threatening for entertainment.—Ntozake Shange
>
> I look at pornography as a system and practice of prostitution, as evidence of women's second class status. It is a central feature of patriarchal society. —Norma Ramos
>
> Pornography is the graphic, sexually explicit subordination of women that includes one of a series of scenarios, from women being dehumanized—turned into objects and commodities—through women showing pleasure in being raped, through the dismemberment in a way that makes the dismemberment sexual. —Andrea Dworkin[6]

Radical feminism's current definition of pornography is the logical outgrowth of its view of heterosexual sex, which was well expressed over a decade ago by Andrea Dworkin. Throughout her still-classic book *Pornography: Men Possessing Women*, Dworkin's diatribe on men and heterosexuality borders on hate-mongering. "Men develop a strong loyalty to violence. Men must come to terms with violence because it is the prime component of male identity." (p. 51) "The immutable self of the male boils down to an utterly unselfconscious parasitism." (p. 13) "Men are distinguished from women by their commitment to do violence rather than to be victimized by it." (p. 53) "Men want women to be objects, controllable as objects are controllable." (p. 65)[7]

Dworkin's 1988 book, *Letters from a War Zone*, continues this theme by presenting marriage as prostitution and romance as rape.

The bridge linking these two positions—the rejection of heterosexuality and the definition of pornography as violence—was forged in 1983 with the proposed Minneapolis Anti-Pornography Ordinance. This remains the touchstone definition used by the anti-porn forces. Because it was a watershed, I quote it in full:

> (gg) *Pornography.* Pornography is a form of discrimination on the basis of sex. (1) Pornography is the sexually explicit subordination of women, graphically depicted, whether in pictures or in words, that also includes one or more of the following:
>
> (i) women are presented as dehumanized sexual objects, things or commodities; or
>
> (ii) women are presented as sexual objects who enjoy pain or humiliation; or
>
> (iii) women are presented as sexual objects who experience sexual pleasure in being raped; or
>
> (iv) women are presented as sexual objects tied up or cut up or mutilated or bruised or physically hurt; or
>
> (v) women are presented in postures of sexual submission; [or sexual servility, including by inviting penetration] or
>
> (vi) women's body parts—including but not limited to vaginas, breasts, and buttocks—are exhibited, such that women are reduced to those parts; or
>
> (vii) women are presented as whores by nature; or
>
> (viii) women are presented being penetrated by objects or animals; or
>
> (ix) women are presented in scenarios of degrada-

> tion, injury, abasement, torture, shown as filthy or inferior, bleeding, bruised, or hurt in a context that makes these conditions sexual.[8]

Several aspects of this definition cannot pass without comment. First, the set-up to this analysis of pornography baldly and stipulatively defines it as "discrimination based on sex" and the "sexually explicit subordination of women." This is not a definition; it is a conclusion, and one which is offered without argument or evidence.

Next, the specific images that constitute pornography are described in extremely subjective and value-laden terms, such as "dehumanized," "humiliation," "degradation," and "whores by nature." What do these terms mean? Humiliation means something different to every single woman. And short of a woman's waving a handful of cash while having sex, it is difficult to even imagine what the phrase "whore by nature" means.

Moreover, some of the images covered by the definition go far beyond what can reasonably be considered pornographic. For example, "women's body parts . . . are exhibited such that women are reduced to those parts." This description would include everything from blue jean commercials which zoom in on women's asses to cream ads which show perfectly manicured hands applying the lotion—the sort of advertisements that have appeared in *Ms.* magazine. Although it is commonplace to criticize such ads for using sex to sell products, it is a real stretch to call them pornographic.

Further, although pornography is predefined as a form of violence against women, several clauses of this definition have nothing to do with such abuse. Instead, they deal with explicit sexual content—e.g., women as sex objects who "invite penetration." This is more of an attack on heterosexual sex than it is on pornography. After all, if there isn't an "invitation to penetration," how can the man know that consent is present?

Other clauses merely refer to images that reflect specific erotic preferences, such as buttocks or breasts.

The ordinance's definition goes far beyond defining pornography, and well into mandating what is sexually correct to see, hear, and express.

PORNOGRAPHY VERSUS EROTICA

Words define the parameters of debate. They control thought itself. George Orwell described this process as NewSpeak in his book *1984*, which described a totalitarian societal nightmare. The ultimate goal of NewSpeak was to construct a language such that it was impossible to utter an "incorrect" sentence.

Part of the anti-porn attempt to control the debate has been the forced distinction they've drawn between pornography and erotica. Basically, pornography is nasty; erotica is healthy. What exactly constitutes erotica is never clearly expressed. It is merely described as life-affirming, while pornography is decried as degrading.

In the book *Confronting Pornography*, Jill Ridington offers her dividing line between the two types of sexual expression:

"If the message is one that equates sex with domination, or with the infliction of pain, or one that denies sex as a means of human communication, the message is a pornographic one. . . . Erotica, in contrast, portrays mutual interaction."[9]

Is there a real distinction between pornography and erotica? And why does it matter?

Let me draw a parallel. A friend and I have a pleasant disagreement about whether there is a distinction between science fiction and fantasy. These two types of writing are often lumped together, with many books combining elements of both. Although the debate may be fruitless, it is good-natured and of no great consequence.

Not so with the current mania for distinguishing between

erotica and pornography. The debate over where to draw the line between these two forms of literature is anything but good-natured. When that line is drawn, those who fall on the wrong side of it may well be arrested and imprisoned by those who control the definitions.

The entire process resembles a scene from Lewis Carroll's *Alice in Wonderland*:

> "When I use a word," Humpty Dumpty said, in a rather scornful tone, "it means just what I choose it to mean—neither more nor less."
>
> "The question is," said Alice, "whether you *can* make words mean so many different things."
>
> "The question is," said Humpty Dumpty, "which is to be master—that's all."

Humpty Dumpty was engaging in making what has been called "stipulative definitions"—namely, the sort of definition which makes the word mean anything you want it to. For example, arbitrarily redefining pornography from common usage—"sex books and sex movies"—to the sexually correct meaning of "an act of rape."

Fortunately, some feminists, like Joanna Russ in *Magic Mommas, Trembling Sisters, Puritans and Perverts,* are applying common sense rather than ideology to this distinction:

"Until recently I assumed . . . that 'art' is better than 'pornography' just as 'erotica' is one thing and 'pornography' another; and just as 'erotica' surpasses 'pornography,' so 'art' surpasses 'erotica.' I think we ought to be very suspicious of these distinctions insofar as they are put forward as moral distinctions."[10]

With such a Wonderland of definitions floating about, it is prudent to take a step backward and ask, What constitutes a proper definition of anything?

DEFINING A DEFINITION

At the risk of sounding like an instructor of Logic 101, let me run the word *pornography* through a definitional process.

A good definition consists of two basic components:

The *definiendum*. This is the word or concept being defined. In the tentative definition "pornography is sexually explicit literature," the term *pornography* is the definiendum;

The *definiens*. This is the defining part of the definition. In "pornography is sexually explicit literature," the phrase "sexually explicit literature" is the definiens.

The process of defining a word involves analyzing it in several ways:

What is the *genus*? That is, what is the general class or category to which the word belongs? In "*pornography* is sexually explicit literature," the term *literature* is the genus. It is the wider category to which *pornography* belongs. Once the broad context for *pornography* has been established, the process of definition becomes a matter of narrowing things down. The next question becomes:

What is the *differentia*? That is, what distinguishes *pornography*—from all other forms of literature? What essential characteristics make pornography different from murder mysteries or historical novels?

Establishing the differentia means following certain rules, the most basic of which are:

1. The essential characteristics—or the common denominator found in all instances of the definiendum—cannot be too broad. Consider the definition "human beings are animals that walk on two legs." Since gorillas also walk on two legs, this differentia is too broad.

2. The essential characteristics should not be too narrow. Thus, "human beings are animals that negoti-

ate contracts" is too narrow because it excludes those people who have never signed a contract.

To state these two principles in one sentence: The definition should apply to all possible cases, and only to those cases.

By these standards, definitions can be regarded as either true or false. Competing definitions can be evaluated as better or worse.

WHAT IS PORNOGRAPHY?

I propose a value-neutral definition: *Pornography is the explicit artistic depiction of men and/or women as sexual beings.* The modifier *explicit* excludes such gray areas as women's romance novels. The modifier *artistic* distinguishes pornography from psychological analyses of sex, such as those found in Freudian textbooks. The term *depiction* includes a wide range of expression, including paintings, literature, and videos. Thus, the genus of my definition of pornography is "the explicit artistic depiction."

The differentia is "of men and/or women as sexual beings." This means that pornography is the genre of art or literature which focuses on the sexual nature of human beings. This does not mean pornography cannot present people as full well-rounded human beings. *But,* in order for the piece of art to be part of the "genre" of pornography, it must explicitly emphasize their sexuality.

Two things are missing from my definition of *pornography* which are generally found elsewhere. It is common to refer to pornography as "material intended to sexually arouse"; I have excluded the intention of the author or producer. I have also excluded the reaction of the reader or viewer.

In other words, I claim that *The Tropic of Cancer* is inherently pornographic, quite apart from Henry Miller's intentions. To put this in another way: What if Miller protested that he was doing a political commentary on fascism, not a piece of pornography? Would his intention somehow convert the book into a work of political science? By my definition, no. *The Tropic of Cancer* would be a work of pornography whether or not Miller had hoped to achieve something else.

Equally, what if a reader became tremendously aroused by *Animal Farm* and not at all by Miller's book? The reader's response would not alter the fact that Miller, not Orwell, is the one presenting pornography.

"Pornography is the explicit artistic depiction of men and/or women as sexual beings." This is not merely a working definition. It is a definition I propose as a new and neutral starting point for a more fruitful discussion of pornography.

IS PORNOGRAPHY GOOD OR BAD?

With a working definition in place, it is possible to move on to the next question, Is pornography good or bad? This question is usually asked in one of two manners:

1. Is the explicit depiction of sex, *in general,* a good or bad thing?

Opinions on this range widely. At one extreme are the Religious Right and the anti-porn feminists, who condemn any graphic expression of sexuality, including straightforward nudity. At another extreme are those people who view any sexual censorship as being far worse than pornography could ever be. Most people fall in the middle. They tend to judge pornography on a case-by-case basis.

2. Is a *specific* piece of pornography good or bad art?

This is an aesthetic question. It revolves around identifying the major themes being expressed and evaluating how well the themes have been executed.

Most pornography is bad art. Indeed, pornography probably contains less artistic value than any other genre of literature and art. The reason for this is simple. Whenever a genre is stigmatized (or criminalized), the best writers and minds tend to abandon it. Those authors—such as D. H. Lawrence or James Branch Cabell or Henry Miller—who persist in bringing their genius to bear are persecuted without mercy. No wonder the industry is dominated by those who rush to make a quick profit rather than a profound insight.

Nevertheless, I believe the quality of pornography is often maligned. Pornography tends to be judged by the worst examples within the genre. Anti-pornographers do not hold up copies of D. H. Lawrence's *Lady Chatterley's Lover* or Erica Jong's *Fear of Flying*. They choose the most repulsive examples they can find and call them "representative." What other genre could withstand being judged by its poorest instances?

CONCLUSION

To repeat: The definition used in this book is: *Pornography is the explicit artistic depiction of men and/or women as sexual beings.*

No area of human psychology needs exploration and understanding as much as sexuality does. At the turn of the century, Freud revolutionized the world's view of sex. Suddenly, it became a popular topic. It became almost a social duty to discuss and examine sex. Now anti-pornography feminists are trying to turn back the clock and shut women's sexuality away behind the locked doors of political correctness. Their first line of attack is to define the debate in their own terms.

The first line of defense is to flatly reject such maneuvering.

THREE

FEMINISM AND PORN: FELLOW TRAVELERS

"Comstockery is the world's standing joke at the expense of the United States. Europe likes to hear of such things. It confirms the deep-seated conviction of the Old World that America is a provincial place, a second-rate country-town civilization after all."
—George Bernard Shaw

Sexually correct history considers the graphic depiction of sex to be the traditional and immutable enemy of women's freedom. Exactly the opposite is true.

Historically, feminism and pornography have been fellow travelers on the rocky road of unorthodoxy. This partnership was natural, perhaps inevitable. After all, both feminism and pornography flout the conventional notion that sex is necessarily connected to marriage or procreation. Both view women as sexual beings who should pursue their sexuality for pleasure and self-fulfillment. Indeed, most of feminism's demands have been phrased in terms of women's sexuality: equal marriage, lesbianism, birth control, abortion, gender justice. . . .

In the nineteenth century, critics of feminism yelled from

pulpits and soapboxes that feminists were corrupting the sanctity of the family and motherhood. Similar charges were also hurled at pornography, then called "obscenity." A century later, right-wing critics of feminism and pornography sound strangely similar to their early counterparts. Perhaps this sort of criticism endures because it contains truth. Both feminism and pornography *do* call the traditional institutions and assumptions of sexuality into question.

The similarity does not end here. Both feminism and pornography flourish in an atmosphere of tolerance, where questions are encouraged and differing attitudes are respected. Not surprisingly, both feminism and pornography are suppressed whenever sexual expression is regulated.

The current backlash of censorship is an alliance between the Moral Majority (the Right) and the politically correct (the Left). This alliance is threatening the freedom of both women and sexual expression. The Right defines the explicit depiction of sex as evil; the Left defines it as violence against women. The result is the same.

The censorship net has been cast so widely that feminist classics, such as Susan Brownmiller's *Against Our Will*, are in the same peril as such porn icons as *Debbie Does Dallas*. This is inevitable. Both works address the same theme: sexual freedom in a sexually repressive world. They merely arrive at antagonistic conclusions.

Why are feminists linking hands with the Right? Perhaps they believe themselves to be in a position of power, at last. Perhaps they dream of having their view of sex become the status quo.

It is a realistic hope. Radical feminists have been successful in establishing sexual correctness as a form of orthodoxy in the university system, where no one currently dares to question concepts like sexual harassment. The media now censors itself to avoid sexually incorrect references. The workplace has turned into halls of paranoia. Anti-pornography feminists have good reason to believe they have a shot at becoming the new power structure.

Meanwhile, pornography is left as a lonely voice to depict the less popular sexual choices that women have available to them.

Feminists desperately need to reacquaint themselves with their own history. What passes for feminist scholarship these days has too often been filtered through ideology. Feminists must come to terms with two of the important lessons that history has taught over and over again:

1. Censorship—or any sexual repression—inevitably rebounds against women, especially against those women who wish to question their traditional roles. Freedom of sexual expression, including pornography, inevitably creates an atmosphere of inquiry and exploration. This promotes women's sexuality and their freedom.
2. Censorship strengthens the position of those in power. This has never been good news for women, who are economically, politically, and socially among the weakest members of society.

Freedom of speech is the freedom to demand change. It will always benefit those who seek to reform society far more than those who wish to maintain the status quo.

A CAUTIONARY TALE

Recently, some scholars have seemed more receptive to the rather commonsense idea that there could be a connection between sexual liberty and women's rights. They have considered the possibility that denying one may hinder the other. A proximate cause for this may be the much-quoted scholarly book by Judith Walkowitz, which examined the Contagious Disease Acts passed in nineteenth-century Britain.[1] These laws were ostensibly intended to prevent the spread of venereal disease in the military. They were also viewed as a means of protecting women (especially young girls) from prostitution by regulating that profession.

The result was disastrous for poor working women.

In 1864, the British Parliament passed the first of the three statutes collectively known as the Contagious Disease Acts. This law mandated "the sanitary (or surgical) inspection" of women suspected of being prostitutes in specific military areas of southern England and Ireland. Since the Act affected few people—and was only expected to inconvenience whores—it aroused little public comment. People did not seem bothered by the fact that diseased women were confined, while diseased soldiers were returned to duty.

The main difficulty in enforcing the law lay in deciding precisely who was a prostitute and who wasn't. After all, this was a period of history during which servant girls and other laboring women commonly sold their bodies on the side, in order to supplement their starvation wages. The solution: The police were given unlimited power to pick up any and every female they considered suspicious.

In the wake of two other Contagious Disease Acts (1866, 1868), prostitution became virtually a state-run industry. The government issued cards to women who were medically checked out and "registered." Then, they were allowed to work the streets. With unlimited powers of arrest, plainclothes policemen picked up women at random. Often, the police proceeded on the basis of gossip or reports from people who had grudges. Women who refused to be surgically examined could be detained at the magistrate's discretion and imprisoned at hard labor. Of course, a well-placed bribe or sexual favor could work miracles.

In the guise of protecting vulnerable women, the law created card-carrying prostitutes, who were at the mercy of the authorities. Girls who used to worry about white slavers now dreaded being sexually abused by the police.

Then, a thunderbolt rocked the prim and hypocritical Victorian world. W. T. Stead's exposé of child prostitution in London appeared in the *Pall Mall Gazette* in the summer of 1885. His ensuing book on the same subject, *The Five Pound Virgin*, so electrified public opinion that a demonstration in Hyde Park drew an estimated 250,000 people. They demanded that the age of consent for girls be raised from thirteen to sixteen. This was part of a growing "social-purity" campaign, which focused on youthful sexuality.

In this campaign, feminists stood side-by-side with those who had been their loudest critics, Anglican bishops. There was no question: Hideous sexual abuses were occurring. But the solution that evolved did not punish those who forced women or girls into prostitution; it regulated the women who were in the profession. Police yanked suspected prostitutes off the street at will, and subjected them to humiliating internal exams.

Such methods lead to the conclusion that the state wanted to control women, rather than to protect them. (This is similar to the situation with pornography today, where the thrust is not to prosecute the individuals who truly coerce women, but to regulate the industry. This is not protection; it is control.)

The Criminal Law Amendment Bill of 1885 raised the age of consent—for girls only!—to sixteen. It also gave police summary jurisdiction over impoverished working women and girls, who could be asked at any moment to prove they were not prostitutes. A difficult task, at best.

The bill was used to control the "bad" habits of the working class, especially their social and sexual habits. For example, under the Bill, "fairs" were banned. These were traditional entertainments where working class men and women socialized freely. The fairs were said to ruin girls, who then brought disease and immorality into the well-to-do homes where they worked as servants.

The social-purity crusade was essentially conservative in nature. It represented a retreat from earlier progress toward women's sexual freedom and equality. Yet few reformers raised so much as a whisper against this brutalization of working-class women.

The French radical Yves Guyot could not understand how anyone who believed women were capable of determining their own best interests could dictate to those who "erred." He remarked: "It is no less strange that many of the very women who have braved insult and calumny in demanding these rights were among the first and loudest supporters of the measure for their furthest restriction."[2]

A century later, Judith Walkowitz asked a similar question: "Why did male and female repealers, who were advocates of personal rights, anti-statist in their political ideology, and even knowledgeable of the realities of working-class prostitution, permit themselves to be swept up in a movement with such repressive political implications?"[3]

An equally good question is: Why are reformers doing so now?

A CASE OF SEXUALLY INCORRECT HISTORY

Anti-pornography feminists need not look across an ocean to find dramatic confirmation of the relationship between sexual freedom and women's rights. Nineteenth-century America provides its own cautionary tale.

In the social turbulence following the Civil War, thousands of men and women enlisted in a purity campaign. They sought to establish a single standard of sexual morality for both sexes. This was not a drive for greater freedom; it was a puritanical campaign to narrow the choices of individuals down to socially acceptable ones.

These crusaders considered a free and open sexuality to be a reflection of the selfish appetites of men, who disrespected women. After all, women were naturally chaste. They were the

mothers and the wives and the cornerstone of the church. Purity
—the curbing of men's appetites—required social control. Thus,
the purity crusaders rallied for laws against prostitution, alcohol,
and pornography—then called obscenity.

Many female and male reformers climbed on the purity band
wagon. In doing so, they destroyed a small but growing feminist
movement. That movement was virtually the only voice of its
time crying out for women's sexual rights. It focused on the twin
goals of marriage reform and the distribution of birth control.

The story of how this movement was coldly killed is one of the
most tragic episodes in feminist history. Yet it has been virtually
ignored by modern feminist scholars. The tale is as follows:

By 1865—the year the Civil War ended—the U.S. Congress
had adopted its first law barring obscenity from the U.S. mails.
The mailing of obscenity was officially declared to be a criminal
offense. But there was an enforcement problem: The post office
had no legal right to refuse to deliver anything. Penalties could be
imposed only after the obscene material had gone through the
mail. This was awkward, both legally and tactically.

In 1868, the New York branch of the Young Men's Christian
Association (YMCA) began to urge the state legislature to outlaw
"the traffic in obscenity" in order to keep corrupting material
out of the hands of impressionable young men. In this cause, the
YMCA found a zealous champion named Anthony Comstock.

Born in 1844, Comstock was one of ten children—three of
whom died before reaching majority. One might think this background would make Comstock pro-birth control. But Comstock
was deeply religious and seemed to blame man's animal nature,
rather than poor medical techniques, for his family's tragedies.

A passionate rejection of sexuality led Comstock to attack the
dime novels, popular in his day, as "devil-traps for the young."
Indeed, one of his early slogans was "Books Are Feeders for
Brothels."

Affluent members of the YMCA provided their crusader with an annual salary of $3,000 plus expenses. This allowed him to quit his employment as a dry-goods clerk and devote full time to anti-obscenity work.

Comstock spent his days tracking down those who dealt in books that offended him. Then, he arranged for their arrest. But his jurisdiction extended only to the borders of New York State. To get at the publishers of obscenity—the source of the vileness! —Comstock needed a federal law that let him cross state lines. In 1872, the Committee for the Suppression of Vice was founded in New York, with Comstock as its agent. (The "Committee" later became the "Society.") Together with the YMCA, the Committee pushed for a sweeping federal law.

Comstock went to Washington, D.C., where he vigorously lobbied in the halls of Congress. Like some current anti-pornography crusaders, Comstock carried pornographic displays with him, with which he shocked and manipulated people's sensibilities. He must have put on a good show, because what came to be known as the Comstock Act passed at two a.m. Sunday March 2, 1873. The Act was pushed through in a rowdy closing session of Congress, with less than one hour of debate.

Through this legislation, Congress amended the United States criminal code to prohibit the transport by public mail of material that included the following:

> . . . [A]ny obscene book, pamphlet, paper, writing, advertisement, circular, print, picture, drawing or other representation, figure, or image on or of paper or other material, or any cast, instrument or other article of an immoral nature, or any drug or medicine, or any article whatever, for the prevention of conception, or for unlawful abortion, or . . . advertise same for sale. . . .[4]

Birth control information was now obscene. The Act provided for up to ten years' imprisonment for anyone who knowingly mailed or received such "obscene, lewd, or lascivious" printed and graphic material.

A series of state laws modeled on the federal one quickly ensued. Every state but New Mexico took some form of action. Twenty-four states passed legislation that banned contraceptive information and devices from the public mails, *and* from being circulated through private publication. Fourteen states banned speech on the subject. Connecticut prohibited people from using birth control. Collectively, these became known as the Comstock laws.

Meanwhile, the post office assumed independent powers of censorship and confiscation. *And* Congress appointed Comstock as a special agent of the post office to inspect mail and to hunt down those who violated federal standards of what was mailable. The Society for the Suppression of Vice—which Comstock headed until his death in 1915—received a large chunk of every fine collected from these prosecutions.

Using blatant entrapment, the purity crusader racked up a large list of "victories." With no due process, postal officials confiscated, refused to accept, or simply destroyed any mail they didn't like. Postmaster General Wanamaker interpreted "obscenity" in very broad terms indeed: For example, he declared a book by the Christian pacifist Leo Tolstoy to be obscene. Comstock's major target, however, was contraception, which he associated with prostitution.

Comstock zealously pursued birth control advocates. Using false signatures, he wrote decoy letters which asked for information. These letters appealed to the sympathy of doctors and reformers in order to entrap them. At one point, he arrested a woman doctor for selling him a syringe to be used for birth control—a syringe that was legally available in any drugstore. By January 1874, Comstock had traveled 23,500 miles by rail, seized

194,000 obscene pictures and photos, 134,000 pounds of books, 14,200 stereo plates, 5,500 decks of playing cards, had made 55 arrests, secured 20 convictions, and seized 60,300 "obscene rubber items."

Soon, he started to run out of birth control advocates to persecute. Reformers fell silent rather than become targets. Books that discussed birth control before 1873 simply removed these sections from later editions. Even periodicals which were sympathetic to women's sexual rights refused to back birth control in print.

Those brave enough to protest Comstock's methods were ignored. For example, in February 1878, the influential Liberal League presented Congress with a petition 2,100 feet long bearing 70,000 names. It protested the Comstock Act. The petition was tabled.

Many of the Comstock laws are still in force today. Contraception was not removed from the postal prohibition list until 1971, after four years of effort by Representative James H. Scheuer of New York. He became involved in this cause when a U.S. customs officer made one of Scheuer's constituents throw her diaphragm into the harbor before allowing her to re-enter the country.

The real tragedy of the Comstock laws is best appreciated by looking at how it devastated the lives of the brave reformers—both male and female—who tried to better the lot of women.

THE BACKGROUND OF SEXUAL REPRESSION

For most of the nineteenth century, women were the chattel of their husbands. Men had legal title to their wives' property and wages, to children, and even to their wives' bodies. Women could be locked away in insane asylums at the discretion of their husbands or other male relatives. They had no voice in government. They could not enter into contracts without their husband's consent. Even labor unions shut out the most needy of workers:

women. Those seats of enlightenment—the universities—locked their doors against women who dared to ask for knowledge.

To be a woman was to be powerless.

Before the Civil War, a vibrant feminist movement arose to address the abysmal condition of women.

Feminism in America, as an organized self-conscious force, grew out of the abolitionist movement of the 1830s. Here women played prominent roles as lecturers, writers, and political organizers. Abolitionism was the radical anti-slavery movement that demanded an immediate cessation to slavery on the grounds that every human being is a self-owner. In other words, every human being has moral jurisdiction over his or her own body.

Abolitionist women began to ask themselves how much better off they were than slaves. The anti-slavery feminist Abbie Kelly observed: "We have good cause to be grateful to the slave, for the benefit we have received to ourselves, in working for him. In striving to strike his irons off, we found most surely that we were manacled ourselves."[5]

And, in case anyone missed the parallel being drawn between slavery and the condition of women, the Grimke sisters—Sarah and Angelina—explicitly compared the two. Sarah began by quoting the foremost legal authority of the day, Judge Blackstone, who declared: "If the wife be injured in her person or property, she can bring no action for redress without her husband's concurrence, and in his name as well as her own.' "

Sarah went on to observe: "[T]his law is similar to the law respecting slaves: 'A slave cannot bring suit against his master or any other person for an injury—his master must bring it.' "

Sarah also compared a Louisiana law that said everything possessed by a slave belonged to his master with a law that said, "A woman's personal property by marriage becomes absolutely her husband's which, at his death, he may leave entirely from her."[6]

The issue that united the anti-slavery and feminist movements was a demand for the right of every human being to control *his or her* own body and property. This same principle is the core of individualist feminism today.

The Civil War derailed the drive for women's rights. Women were explicitly asked to put aside their own complaints and fight for a larger cause: freedom for the slaves through victory for the North. After the War, when the Fourteenth and Fifteenth Amendments to the Constitution passed Congress, women were left out in the political cold. The Fourteenth Amendment ensured the right to vote to every law-abiding *male* American (excluding Native Americans). The Fifteenth Amendment assured that the right to vote could not be abridged because of "race, color, or previous condition of servitude." Not sex. Women were omitted from both Amendments.

From this point onward, feminists tended to take one of three paths toward women's rights. The mainstream reformers worked for woman's suffrage. Some radical women worked for social change as expressed through "social-purity crusades"—e.g., raising the age of consent, the reformation of prostitutes, and the censorship of obscenity. In *Woman's Body, Woman's Right*, Linda Gordon commented on this period: "The closer we look, the harder it is to distinguish social-purity groups from feminist ones. Feminists from very disparate groups were advocates of most major social purity issues. . . ."[7]

Abolitionist feminists had also believed in purity, but for them it had to emerge from the purity of an individual's conscience; social-purity feminists seemed quite willing to enforce morality by law.

Other radicals fought for sexual rights, for freedom rather than for purity. This movement offered an ideological home for those who believed in self-ownership: a woman's body, a woman's right. It was called free love.

The free-love movement is best remembered by a witticism from the twentieth-century radical Emma Goldman. When asked if she believed in free love, Emma retorted, "I certainly don't believe in paying for it." The theory of free love, however, is a bit more complicated than this response implies.

The philosophy of free love has no connection with promiscuity. For example, the banner flying over a nineteenth-century free-love community in Ohio proclaimed, "Freedom, Fraternity, Chastity." Why was such a chaste community considered a haven for free-lovers? Because it lived by the principle that no coercion should exist in sexual relations between adults. Free-lovers vehemently denied the state had any right to intervene in the sexual arrangements of consenting adults. They focused on empowering the weakest and most abused partner in sex: the woman.

There were two keys to securing sexual rights for women. The first was to reform the marriage laws, which gave husbands almost absolute authority over their wives. Marriage—free-lovers insisted—should be a voluntary and equal association between two people who shared a spiritual affinity.

The second key was access to birth control information and devices.

As Comstock tried to push the door closed on women's sexuality, the free-love movement tried to take that door off its hinges. Although it is not politically correct to acknowledge the fact, two of the most courageous figures in the fight for women's freedom were white males: Ezra Heywood and Moses Harman. Both men were destroyed because they tried to help women.

The Heywoods and The Word

Ezra H. Heywood was an abolitionist and an outspoken advocate for women's rights. In 1865, he married Angela Fiducia Tilton. Although they were a devoted couple with four children, Ezra and Angela became convinced that marriage was the single greatest obstacle to true love. Indeed, the Heywoods considered traditional marriage to be prostitution. They reasoned: Men had reduced women to such socioeconomic dependence that, in order to live, the women were forced to chose between selling their labor for next to nothing or selling their bodies into unwanted unions.

In 1872, Ezra launched his periodical, *The Word*, from Princeton, Massachusetts, as a vehicle for labor reform. The Prospectus of *The Word* declared, "THE WORD favors the abolition of speculative income, of women's slavery, and war government. . . ." Almost from the beginning, *The Word* had a wide circulation with subscribers in every state of the union, as well as internationally. The Heywoods began with the declared intention of rescuing women from economic subordination; but, slowly, *The Word* was drawn deeper and deeper into the free-love issue. Soon, it began to focus on sexual freedom in a direct and candid manner that can be directly attributed to Angela.

Angela's style was a strange blend of flowery language and a no-holds-barred bluntness. Although she wrote with an idealistic flourish, she did not blush at using the word *fuck* in print. Angela shocked nineteenth-century sensibilities when she wrote, "Sexuality is a divine ordinance elegantly natural from an eye-glance to the vital action of the penis and womb, in personal exhilaration or for reproductive uses."

As for women's pleasure, she insisted that if a woman "duly gives to man who cometh in unto her, as freely, as equally, as well as he give her, how shall she be abashed or ashamed of the innermost?" Angela also provided what is perhaps the first defense of abortion solely on the basis of self-ownership, thus breaking intellectual ground for the principle "a woman's body, a woman's right."[8]

The Heywoods established The Co-operative Publishing Company, from which they launched a full frontal attack on marriage. In 1873, they founded the New England Free Love League and began to date their correspondence and writings with the chronological designation Y.L., "Year of Love."

In 1873, The Co-operative Publishing Company put out a pamphlet entitled *Uncivil Liberty*, which had been written by Ezra, with Angela's active assistance. It called for women's suffrage and argued that the political enfranchisement of women would lead to the social emancipation of both sexes. Eighty thousand copies of the pamphlet were distributed.

Then, in 1876, the Company put out another pamphlet entitled *Cupid's Yokes*, subtitled *The Binding Forces of Conjugal Life: An Essay to Consider Some Moral and Physiological Phases of Love and Marriage, Wherein Is Asserted the Natural Right and Necessity of Sexual Self-Government*. The distribution of this twenty-three-page essay has been estimated variously at from fifty thousand to two hundred thousand. The term "Cupid's Yokes" referred to the healthy ties of love that should replace a legal certificate as the true evidence of marriage. Ezra also argued for birth control and called for the immediate repeal of the Comstock laws. He even ridiculed the august Anthony Comstock as "a religious monomaniac."

Indeed, Ezra seemed to delight in ridiculing Comstock. At one point, *The Word* offered a contraceptive device for sale—a vaginal-douche syringe—which was called the Comstock syringe.

Using the false name of E. Edgewell, Comstock wrote to the Heywoods and ordered a copy of *Cupid's Yokes* to entrap the editor. This was one of a series of letters that Comstock addressed to Ezra.

On November 3, 1877, while speaking in Boston, Ezra was personally arrested by Comstock. The purity crusader recorded his reaction at having to sit in the audience, listening to the meeting's proceedings, while he awaited the right moment to bag his prize:

"I could see lust in every face. . . . The wife of the president [Ezra] (the person I was after) took the stand, and delivered the foulest address I ever heard. She seemed lost to all shame. The audience cheered and applauded. It was too vile; I had to go out."[9]

Ezra was charged with circulating obscene material through the mail. At the commencement of the trial, the prosecution held that *Cupid's Yokes* was too obscene to be placed upon the records of the court. Thus, the obscenity of the pamphlet was assumed when the trial started. The court also forbade any investigation into the purpose or merits of the work, as well as any medical or scientific testimony.

On June 25, 1878, Ezra Heywood was sentenced to pay a $100 fine and to be confined for two years at hard labor. On August 1, six thousand people demonstrated in Faneuil Hall in Boston. They demanded the editor's release and the repeal of the Comstock laws. After serving six months, Ezra was released under a special pardon from President Hayes. Comstock was outraged; he renewed his determination to stop *Cupid's Yokes* from circulating.

His next target became D. M. Bennett—editor of the freethought periodical *Truth Seeker*—who flouted the Comstock laws by advertising *Cupid's Yokes*.

The Bennett case—*U.S.* versus *Bennett* (1879)[10]—rewrote American obscenity law, because it introduced the Hicklin standard to American jurisprudence. The Hicklin standard for obscenity derived from a decision in the British court case *Regina* versus *Hicklin* (1868).[11] Under this standard, anything that tended to "deprave and corrupt those whose minds are open to such immoral influences" was considered to be obscene. The Hicklin standard would remain the basis of American obscenity law for more than half a century.

Persecutions only made Ezra harden his stand. In 1882, he was again arrested for distributing *Cupid's Yokes* along with other "obscene" materials, including two of Walt Whitman's poems. He was acquitted on April 12, 1883, then quickly arrested again for distributing an essay written by Angela, which argued for birth control.

This obscenity charge, along with one in 1887, was never prosecuted, largely due to public protest. Then, in 1890, *The Word* reprinted a letter from the free-love periodical *Lucifer, the Light Bearer*—a letter which had occasioned the trial of *Lucifer*'s editor, Moses Harman, on charges of mailing obscenity.

Heywood was arrested and indicted on three counts of obscenity. He was sentenced to two years at hard labor, which he served in its entirety. Released in poor health, Ezra Heywood died a year later, on May 22, 1893, after catching a cold.

The Word ceased publication. It had been killed by those who sought to control sexual expression.

It was left to Moses Harman, publisher of *Lucifer, the Light Bearer*, and the circle of courageous reformers who gathered about him, to continue the fight for women's sexual rights.

The Lucifer Circle

On a hot June Sunday in 1879, the widower Moses Harman and his two children, George and Lillian, arrived in the sleepy midwestern town of Valley Falls, Kansas. The small town would become a center of sexual reform in America. Although his neighbors must have initially approved of Harman's respectable appearance and well-mannered ways, they soon saw a more controversial side of the man. For Moses Harman was an uncompromising crusader for free love and against what he labeled the Twin Despots: the paternalistic state and the church.

In his private life, Harman was something of a prude, but he insisted that everyone be free to make decisions concerning sex without requiring permission from a church or the state. In particular, he demanded uncontrolled access to birth control, and marriage by contract.

In 1883, Harman began publishing a periodical entitled *Lucifer, the Light Bearer* (1883–1907). The paper was so named because it was Lucifer, not God, who offered man the knowledge of good and evil. Like Prometheus, Lucifer brought light to man; like Prometheus, he became an outcast for doing so. Lucifer was the first political rebel; he questioned the status quo of authority called God.

Lucifer quickly became the outstanding journal of sexual liberty of its day. It almost defined the limits of sexual freedom in late nineteenth-century America.

Lucifer also became a prime target of Anthony Comstock, who bristled at the periodical's open discussion of birth control, and of forced marital sex as rape. Although Harman knew the risk involved in addressing such issues, he maintained: "Words are not deeds, and it is not the province of civil law to take preventative measures against remote or possible consequences of words, no matter how violent or incendiary."[12]

On February 23, 1887, a federal marshal arrived in Valley Falls to arrest the staff of *Lucifer* on 270 counts of obscenity, which resulted from its publication of four letters to the editor. The number of counts was somewhat arbitrary, since *Lucifer* was considered too obscene to be read before a judge or jury. Harman responded by reprinting the letters along with a passage from the Old Testament, which portrayed incest, harlotry, and coitus interruptus. He did this in the hope of having the Bible declared obscene. (His efforts came to naught. Not until 1895, when J. B. Wise mailed a postcard inscribed with a salty verse, was the Bible declared legally obscene.)

The charges sprang from a policy Moses Harman had initiated in the spring of 1886. Harman vowed not to edit letters sent to *Lucifer* because of the language they contained. Although Harman did not agree with everything he printed, he thought free speech vented whatever evil lay in the hearts of men and women.

In the June 18 issue, a letter appeared from a Tennessee doctor, W. G. Markland. Because of its historical importance the Markland letter is quoted here extensively:

> EDS. LUCIFER: To-day's mail brought me a letter from a dear lady friend, from which I quote and query:
> "About a year ago F——— gave birth to a babe, and was severely torn by the use of instruments in incompetent hands. She has gone through three operations and all failed. I brought her home and had Drs. ———and———operate on her, and she was getting along nicely until last night, when her husband came down, forced himself into her bed and the stitches were torn from her healing flesh, leaving her in a worse condition than ever. I don't know what to do. . . .
> Laws are made for the protection of life, person and property.
> Will you point to a law that will punish this brute?
> Was his conduct illegal? The marriage license was a permit of the people at large given by their agent for this man and woman—a mere child—to marry.
> Marry for what? Business? That he may have a housekeeper? He could legally have hired her for that. Save one thing, is there anything a man and woman can do for each other which they may not legally do without marrying?
> Is not that one thing copulation? Does the law interfere in any other relations of service between the sexes?
> What is rape? Is it not coition with a woman by force, not having a legal right?
> Can there be legal rape? Did this man rape his wife?

Would it have been rape had he not been married to her?

Does the law protect the person of woman in marriage? Does it protect her person out of marriage?

Does not the question of rape turn on the pivot of legal right regardless of consequences?

If a man stabs his wife to death with a knife, does not the law hold him for murder?

If he murders her with his penis, what does the law do?

If the wife, to protect her life, stabs her husband with a knife, does the law hold her guiltless?

Can a Czar have more absolute power over a subject than a man has over the genitals of his wife?

Is it not a fearful power? Would a kind, considerate husband feel robbed, feel his manhood emasculated, if deprived of this legal power?

Does the safety of society depend upon a legal right which none but the coarse, selfish, ignorant brutal will assert and exercise? . . .

Has freedom gender? . . ."

W. G. Markland[13]

The second offending letter was a protest against contraceptives on the grounds that they removed an obstacle to husbands who wished to have sex: namely, the fear of another mouth to feed. The third letter retold an anecdote about a couple who thought the world was ending and, therefore, told each other about their sexual improprieties. A fourth one discussed the relative virtues of two methods of sexual abstinence.

For these obscenities, Moses and his son George were arrested. All charges were later dropped against George.

On February 14, 1890, the unrepentant *Lucifer* printed a letter from a New York physician that detailed the sexual abuses he had seen in the course of his practice. The doctor's graphic accounts included a description of a man who liked to perform oral sex on other men. The letter remains one of the few nineteenth-century journalistic discussions of oral sex.

Moses Harman was sentenced to serve five years in prison and to pay a $300 fine. After serving seventeen weeks, he was released on a technicality, retried without a jury on a slightly different charge, and sentenced to one year. After eight months, he was again released on a technicality.

The renowned British playwright George Bernard Shaw lamented Harman's plight in a front-page interview in *The New York Times*:

". . . A journal has just been confiscated and its editor imprisoned in America for urging that a married woman should be protected from domestic molestation when childbearing. Had that man filled his paper with aphrodisiac pictures and aphrodisiac stories of duly engaged couples, he would be a prosperous, respected citizen."[14]

Harman continued to be persecuted through the Comstock laws, even though few people believed his periodical contained anything obscene. On one occasion, for example, the postal authorities objected to the sentence, "it is natural and reasonable that a prospective mother should be exempt from the sexual relation during gestation." Ironically, this sentence had been excerpted from a book by a noted doctor, E. B. Foote—a book which was allowed to circulate freely in the mails.

Harman's last imprisonment for obscenity was in 1906, when he was seventy-five years old. Moses was sentenced to a year at hard labor in Joliet. When breaking rocks for eight-and-a-half hours a day in the bitter winter cold threatened his health, his friends pressured the authorities and managed to get him transferred.

At about this time, Shaw was asked why he did not visit America. He answered bluntly:

The reason I do not go to America is that I am afraid of being arrested by Mr. Anthony Comstock and imprisoned like Mr. Moses Harman.... If the brigands can, without any remonstrance from public opinion, seize a man of Mr. Harman's advanced age, and imprison him for a year under conditions which amount to an indirect attempt to kill him, simply because he shares the opinion expressed in my *Man and Superman* that 'marriage is the most licentious of human institutions,' what chance should I have of escaping?

No thank you; no trips to America for me.[15]

The last issue of *Lucifer*—brought out by Moses's daughter Lillian—was a tribute to her father, who died in 1908. But the eulogy I have always preferred was published in 1891, by a woman who subscribed to *Lucifer*. She called the periodical "the cry of women in pain":

It is the mouthpiece, almost the only mouthpiece in the world, of every poor, suffering, defrauded, subjugated woman. Many know they suffer, and cry out in their misery, though not in the most grammatical of sentences.... A simple woman ... may know nothing of her biology, psychology, or of the evolution of the human race, but she knows when she is forced into a relation disagreeable or painful to her. Let her express her pain; the scientists may afterwards tell why she suffers, and what are the remedies, —if they can.[16]

Censorship silenced women in pain. It silenced *The Word* and *Lucifer, the Light Bearer*. Today, it seeks to silence women with aberrant sexual preferences, such as bondage or exhibitionism. The result of social purity was sexual ignorance.

The Word and *Lucifer* were far from the only casualties of the anti-obscenity craze. The following is an abridged list, which gives no more than a sense of the extent of persecution:

• Ann Lohman, who performed abortions and dispensed birth control information, was so hounded by Comstock that she committed suicide. He bragged that she was the fifteenth person he had driven to such an end.

• Frederick Hollick, a physician, tried to popularize the rhythm method, but was discouraged from doing so by the Comstock laws.

• Edward Bliss Foote, author of *Radical Remedy in Social Science* (1886), and his son, Edward Bond Foote, published home medical books. The father was arrested in 1874 for mailing a pamphlet which contained contraceptive information. Because of public opinion, Foote was let off with a stiff fine.

• Elizabeth (Elmina) Drake Slenker, an elderly Quaker lady who advocated abstinence was arrested for mailing allegedly obscene material. The purported obscenity had not been published in a periodical, but enclosed within a sealed envelope.

• Lois Waisbrooker, a feminist and editor of the journal *Foundation Principles*, advised a correspondent to divorce a wife he did not love. For this, she was arrested under the Comstock laws.

The list could scroll on and on.

Yet these people will not be found in books of feminist history. It is difficult to imagine honest motives for ignoring the immense and courageous contributions Ezra Heywood and Moses Harman made to the well-being of women.

A Test of Anti-Porn Feminist Honesty

If these ignored radicals were the only people persecuted by social purity laws, then anti-porn feminists could argue they were unaware of an historical connection between sexual freedom and women's rights. But there is at least one woman persecuted by Anthony Comstock of whom no educated feminist can be ignorant: Margaret Sanger.

Sanger first came into conflict with the Comstock laws as a result of her column entitled "What Every Girl Should Know," which ran in the socialist periodical *The Call.* The offending column graphically described venereal disease. In early 1913, Comstock banned it. In place of the column, *The Call* ran an empty box, with the headline "What Every Girl Should Know—Nothing; by order of the U.S. Post Office."

On October 16, 1916, Margaret Sanger opened America's first birth control clinic in a storefront tenement in Brooklyn. Handbills advertising the clinic were printed in English, Yiddish, and Italian. They urged women not to have abortions, but to prevent conception in the first place. On October 26, Sanger was arrested by the vice squad for distributing contraceptive information. Released that afternoon, she re-opened the clinic. This time the police strong-armed the landlord into evicting her and closed the place down.

As Sanger was driven away in a police vehicle, she looked out the back at the crowds of poor women still standing at the door of her clinic. They had come to her for help. Sanger wrote:

"I heard . . . a scream. It came from a woman wheeling a baby carriage, who had just come around the corner, preparing to visit the clinic. She saw the patrol wagon . . . left the baby carriage, rushed through the crowd to the wagon and cried to me: 'Come back and save me!' "[17]

Sanger was sentenced to thirty days in the workhouse. Because the authorities feared she would go on a hunger strike, she served the term in a less harsh and more obscure prison.

In a provocative move, the first issue of her periodical, *Woman Rebel*, announced an intention to disperse contraceptive information. When the postal authorities declared this issue "obscene," Sanger avoided having it confiscated by mailing it in small batches all over the city. As subscriptions poured in, the post office declared five other issues unmailable.

Meanwhile, Sanger prepared a pamphlet entitled *Family Limitation*, which provided contraceptive information. Before it could be published, the federal government indicted her for the August issue of *Woman Rebel*. Facing a possible forty-five years in prison, Sanger fled to England.

Before doing so, she arranged to have copies of *Family Limitation* printed by a radical publisher, who virtually guaranteed himself a jail term. In early 1915, Comstock personally arrested her husband, William Sanger. He was sentenced to thirty days. Ironically, his trial created a backlash of public support for birth control advocates. Fake subpoenas were sold to those who wished to sit in the extremely crowded courtroom. By the time Margaret Sanger returned to the U.S. in 1916, the political climate had changed. She was a cause célèbre and the government prudently refrained from prosecuting her.

CONCLUSION

Sexual freedom—especially pornography, which is sexual free speech—is an integral part of the battle for *women's* freedom. The censoring of sexual words and images does not simply lead to the suppression of women's sexual rights. It is an attempt to control women themselves. For women's rights have traditionally been phrased in terms of their sexuality: marriage, abortion, birth control. To surrender one iota of women's control over their own sexual expression is to deny that it is *their* sexuality in the first place.

Today, both pornography and women's sexuality are victims of sexual correctness.

Anti-porn feminists need look no further back than to the February 1992 Supreme Court of Canada decision in *Butler* v. *Regina*.[18] The *Butler* decision mandated the seizure of pornography by customs on the grounds that such material threatened the safety of women. In praising the decision, which she considers a victory for women, Catharine MacKinnon speculated: "Maybe in Canada, people talk to each other, rather than buy and sell each other as ideas."[19] Customs has used the decision almost exclusively against lesbian, gay, and feminist material.

Unfortunately, to those driven by ideology, history means very little.

Four

A Critique of Anti-Pornography Feminism

If feminism and pornography are naturally fellow travelers, how did they arrive at the ideological impasse that exists today?

THE RISE OF MODERN FEMINISM AND PORNOGRAPHY

World War II drew a generation of women out of the home and into the workforce, where many of them felt a heady independence for the first time in their lives. When the men returned from war, they reclaimed the jobs women had been performing. But women were now accustomed to wider freedom. In 1946, Congress voted for the first time on an Equal Rights Amendment (ERA). The measure was defeated. In 1950 and then again in 1953, the ERA could not get past Congress.

With the economic boom of the fifties, women seemed to turn away from equality toward the contented affluence of owning a home and raising a middle class suburban family. This was the decade of poodle skirts, Pepto-Bismol colored appliances, and hula hoops. Optimism ran rampant and Father Knew Best. Only a decade later, women demanded a redefinition of who they were and what their role in society was.

What happened in between? The sexual revolution.

In the 1960s, pornography flourished as one of a collection of new freedoms that became collectively known as "sexual liberation." Sex had been liberated by a new political awareness. In a groundswell of protest against the Vietnam War, an entire generation questioned the rules and rewards of their parents' world. Young people "dropped-out," pursued alternate lifestyles, and wanted everything to be "meaningful." Drugs seemed to open doors of consciousness; sex lost its aura of guilt and obligation; government lost its automatic authority.

Women rode this crest of social protest into new and dizzy territory. In 1961, President John F. Kennedy established the first Presidential Commission on the Status of Women. Betty Friedan's pioneering book *The Feminine Mystique* (1963) captured the angst of American housewives who were being imprisoned by their roles as wife and mother. The generation they cooked and cleaned for—their daughters and sons—refused to fall into the trap of tradition. Instead, they co-habited, experimented with communal marriages, came out of the closet, and gave birth out of wedlock. They demanded their own voice.

It wasn't long before women realized that not all voices were equal in this new utopia.

In 1965, women activists at a conference of Students for a Democratic Society raised the issue of women's rights. They were appalled by the derision they encountered from their male counterparts. These were men with whom they had protested the Vietnam War; now these same men wanted to relegate women to working the copy machine and warming their beds. In a backlash of anger, the modern feminist movement was born.

In 1966, the National Organization for Women (NOW) was founded. The next year, the first radical feminist group, the New York Radical Women, was established. Although the radicals were in the minority, the loudness of their voices and the flashiness of their tactics drew the media's attention. The Miss America pageant at Atlantic City was sabotaged; bridal fairs in San Francisco and New York were disrupted; there was a mass sit-in at *Ladies Home Journal* to protest the conventional image of women projected by that magazine. Politically, some women began to call out for a cultural revolution.

The public began to perceive the entire movement as militant and intolerant of the traditional roles of women.

Meanwhile, the more moderate and reform-minded feminists were chalking up an impressive list of political successes. Title VII of the Civil Rights Act prohibited sexual discrimination in the private sector (1964). President Lyndon B. Johnson's Executive Order 11375 forbade sexual discrimination in the public sector (1967). The Equal Employment Opportunity Act empowered a commission to take legal action against employers who discriminated on the basis of sex (1972).

On the streets, huge numbers of women were galvanized and united by the abortion issue. Marching down streets, their rallying cry became "a woman's body, a woman's right."

Meanwhile, pornography was also undergoing a transformation, especially in its legal status. In the fifties, the courts still generally used the Hicklin test to judge whether material was pornographic. This test came from *Regina* v. *Hicklin*.[1] By this standard, anything that tended to "deprave and corrupt those whose minds are open to such immoral influences" was considered obscene.

In 1957, the U.S. Supreme Court decided that the Hicklin test restricted freedom of speech. It was replaced as a standard by the ruling on *Roth* v. *the United States*.[2] This ruling declared that something was pornographic if the "dominant theme . . . appeals to the prurient interest" of the average person.

Pornography began to come out into the open. Then, in 1966 —perhaps as a reflection of society's growing tolerance—the standards loosened again. According to the ruling on *Memoirs* v. *Massachusetts*, material was pornographic if: "(a) the dominant

theme of the material taken as a whole appeals to a prurient interest in sex; (b) the material is patently offensive because it affronts
contemporary community standards relating to the description
or representation of sexual matters; and (c) the material is utterly
without redeeming social value."[3]

It is difficult to establish that anything is "utterly without redeeming social value." This qualification provided a legal loop-
hole that pornographers quickly exploited. The late sixties saw a
flowering of adult films and books. Many of them included a
tagged-on social message or a discussion of hygiene, as a way to
skirt prosecution.

As pornography flourished, it became part of the changing
view of sexuality. Sex was no longer tied, with a nooselike knot,
to procreation, marriage, or romance. Pornography presented a
kaleidoscope of sexual possibilities: as pleasure, with a stranger,
as self-exploration, as power, with groups or with another
woman . . .

The old stereotypes of pornography began to fade away. The
caricature of the type of person who enjoyed pornography—
e.g., dirty old men and nervous perverts—was superseded by the
sight of millions of people subscribing to *Playboy*. Couples
viewed pornography together; explicit sex manuals, such as *The
Joy of Sex*, became best-sellers which were prominently stocked
by mainstream bookstores.

This was the democratization of pornography, by which sexual information became available to everyone—not just to the
wealthy or to those willing to live on the sexual fringe. Even
politically aware periodicals like the Berkeley *Barb* took up the
cause of open sexuality. Founded to promote freedom of speech,
the ad section of the *Barb* soon became dominated by sexually
oriented businesses like massage parlors, and by individuals who
placed ads to contact others with similar sexual preferences. Ordinary people seemed to have an insatiable demand for information about sex.

Feminists benefited immeasurably from the opening up of sex. They held rape "speak-outs" and destroyed the myth that only "bad" women were raped. With the moral connection between sex and motherhood severed, feminists could argue effectively for abortion rights. Lesbians came out of the closet. Sexual pleasure became a right—not only for men, but for women as well. And if men did not provide it—well, Germaine Greer's famous photograph with a banana held conspicuously in one hand reminded men that sexual fulfillment was not a request; it was a demand.

But a strange backlash was already underway. Simone de Beauvoir's pivotal book, *The Second Sex* (1953, reissued in 1961), claimed that lesbianism was the embodiment of sexual freedom. Radical feminists tended to agree. They believed that nothing short of a total sexual revolution could free women. In 1970, the organization Radicalesbians was founded; three years later, the first national conference of feminist lesbians took place in Los Angeles, amid media flashbulbs.

More moderate feminists, who wanted to reform the system by gaining access to abortion, for example, became alarmed.

A schism was opening between moderate heterosexual feminists and their more radical lesbian sisters. Betty Friedan—horrified that her work was being used by radicals to attack marriage and the family—warned against the "lavender menace" (lesbianism). Between 1969 and 1971, NOW—the largest feminist organization and a voice for reform, not revolution—virtually purged its gay and lesbian members.

As radical feminists continued to create their own organizations, such as the Redstockings, lesbianism began to resemble a political choice, rather than a sexual one.

THE DECLINE OF FEMINISM
In 1973, feminism won a tremendous victory when the Supreme Court's decision on *Roe* v. *Wade*[4] ensured legal access to abor-

tion. For years, mainstream feminists had focused on the abortion crusade with a single-minded determination. Now, this goal was achieved. The movement needed another issue around which to organize, through which to be galvanized. They found it: a renewed effort to pass a federal Equal Rights Amendment (ERA).

In 1972, forty-nine years after its introduction in Congress, the ERA had passed the House of Representatives and the Senate. But before it could become law, the ERA needed to be ratified by two-thirds of the states. This seemed so easy that some considered it to be a technicality. The deadline of 1979 was seen as ample time.

In March 1978, one hundred thousand demonstrators marched on Washington, D.C., to express their determined support for ratification. A year later, on the streets of Chicago, ninety thousand women marched in support. The ERA began to dominate NOW and the other mainstream vehicles of feminism. But the votes necessary to ratify remained elusive. 1979 came and went; the ERA obtained an extension to June 30, 1982. After another extension, the measure was again brought to Congress. It was 1984.

The defeat of the ERA crushed the spirit of mainstream feminists. They felt discouraged, tired, and betrayed. Women seemed to turn inward and away from politics. They focused on their careers and personal lives. A flood of self-help books told women how to dress for success, how to keep their men, and how to listen to their inner voices. Politically, mainstream feminism faltered.

Radical feminism had never rushed to embrace the ERA. It had viewed the measure as a Band-Aid remedy for the terminal disease of sexual injustice. Moreover, radical feminists had been shunned by NOW, which had been the main engine behind the ERA drive.

Instead, radical feminists had been busy evolving a new political theory based on gender oppression. This is the contention that men as a class oppress women as a class: All men oppress all women. Collectively, male dominance is known as patriarchy, which is a combination of white male culture and capitalism. Only through revolution, only by destroying the present political, social, and cultural structures, can women become free.

Radical feminism presented an integrated philosophy of gender—including a reinterpretation of history, politics, and science. Gradually, the ideology of gender began to dominate the movement. It filled the vacuum left by the ERA debacle.

Perhaps the pivotal book in the development of radical feminism was Kate Millett's *Sexual Politics* (1970), which argued that women had been "confined to the cultural level of animal life" by men who used them as sexual objects and breeding stock.

A series of works expanded upon Millett's theories. In *Psychoanalysis and Feminism* (1974), Juliet Mitchell dovetailed feminism, Marxism, and psychoanalysis. Linda Gordon's anthology, *Woman's Body, Woman's Right* (1976), provided a history of birth control and placed this issue within a radical, socialist context. Through her tremendously influential book, *Against Our Will*, Susan Brownmiller "gave rape its history"—a history that portrayed men as natural rapists. Throughout the seventies radical feminists did the backbreaking labor of creating a new political philosophy.

Elsewhere within feminism, discontent grew. As the eighties dragged on, women became disillusioned with the movement, which they felt no longer addressed their needs. Affirmative action had promised to remedy the twin economic evils: sex segregation in the workplace, and the wage gap, by which women earned far less than men. Both problems remained. No-fault divorce had failed to rescue women from living below the poverty line. Women had not even been liberated from domesticity. Studies showed that modern men did no more housework than their fathers had before them.

The ERA had been a dismal failure. Even abortion was no longer safe under the presidency of Ronald Reagan, who was openly hostile to the procedure. As one of his last acts before leaving office, Reagan filed a "friend of the court" brief that encouraged the Supreme Court to review a challenge to *Roe* v. *Wade.* The Supreme Court complied.

To many women, it looked as though equality had not worked. The apparent rise of domestic violence seemed to prove this. Although FBI crime records (as indicated by the murder rate) did not indicate that violence against women was increasing more than the population growth or the general crime rate, women *felt* less safe.

Suddenly, reports of sexual terror were everywhere in the media: sexual harassment, coercion into pornography, domestic violence, date rape, wife abuse, child abuse. The euphoria of freedom was overshadowed by the paranoia of failure.

Women had fought so hard and had progressed so little. No achievements seemed to endure, and feminists were not in the mood to celebrate past glories. The politics of liberation had failed; it was time for politics of rage.

THE RISE OF RADICAL FEMINISM

To discouraged women, radical feminists offered an analysis of the movement's failure. More importantly, they offered a solution: Reform can never produce justice for women, they maintained. The problems are rooted too deeply for halfway measures to address them adequately. Salvation lay in revolution—a revolution so profound that it extended beyond politics into human sexuality itself.

According to radical feminists, only a fundamental difference between the sexes could explain the perpetual oppression of women. Only an unbreachable schism between the sexes could explain why women are constantly victimized by men.

As to how the gender oppression was maintained—pornography became the primary culprit for radical feminists, who pointed to graphic depictions of bound or abused women in order to explain the incredible staying power of the male power structure.

Pornography offered radical feminists a clear target for their rage, complete with clear moral categories: Men were villains, women were victims. There was a brotherhood of oppressors, a sisterhood of victims. Pornography became the symbol of man's supposedly unquenchable hatred of women.

Meanwhile, in mainstream society, pornography had already fallen on hard times. Without the freewheeling spirit of the sixties, sexual liberation had come under attack. In its 1973 ruling on *Miller* v. *California,* the Supreme Court found:

> [W]e now confine the permissible scope of such regulation to works which depict or describe sexual conduct. That conduct must be specifically defined by the applicable state law, as written or authoritatively construed. A state offense must also be limited to works, which, taken as a whole, appeal to the prurient interest in sex, which portray sexual conduct in a patently offensive way, and which, taken as a whole, do not have serious literary, artistic, political or scientific value.[5]

This became the new standard for judging what was pornography.

Taking advantage of today's growing intolerance and sexual paranoia, radical feminism is using pornography to revive the battle of the sexes. This time it is all-out war, with no prisoners taken.

The rallying point of pornography came at a fortunate moment for radical feminists. They desperately needed a cause to galvanize the movement in much the same manner as abortion had in the sixties. Radical feminists needed a holy crusade around which to rally alienated and angry women. And pornography was perfectly suited. It provided a clear target. It commanded the instant attention of the media, who love to use sex to boost their ratings or circulation. Attacking pornography allowed the media to titillate viewers while remaining socially responsible.

Pornography fits in perfectly with the politics of revenge and the ideology of rage.

THE IDEOLOGY OF RADICAL FEMINISM

A basic tenet of radical feminism's theory of gender oppression is the idea that sex is a social construct. Radical feminists reject what they call "sexual essentialism"—the notion that sex is a natural force. They reject the idea that sex is based on biology or that women have certain natural tendencies.

Even deeply felt sexual preferences, such as heterosexuality, are not matters of biology. They spring from ideology. To argue otherwise, they insist, is to take the side of conservative anti-feminists. It is to accept that biology makes women weaker than men, and slates them for domesticity. Anyone who claims women's sexuality comes from biology is blaming the victims for their own oppression.

The "nature or nurture" argument may be intrinsically interesting, but the most important political question for this debate is rarely voiced. That question is: What difference does it make?

To feminists who advocate "a woman's body, a woman's right," there are no political implications to taking a nature or a nurture stand. Whether a woman's sexuality is formed by genetics, by culture, or by some combination of the two, it is still *her* body and the political significance of this remains unchanged. She is free to do with it whatever she chooses.

Consider a parallel: Everyone's intellect is formed by a combination of biology and cultural influences—including parents, school, books, television, and peer pressure. Yet few people would argue that a woman should not be allowed to think for herself and reach her own conclusions, simply because she has been influenced by her environment. Indeed, a woman's ability to reason and to control her own actions may be her only defense against hostile surroundings.

But, to anti-pornography feminists, the idea that sex is a social construct is good news. If sex has been constructed, it also can be deconstructed and put back together correctly.

The key to deconstructing women's sexuality lies in rejecting all of the male institutions that have defined and oppressed women for centuries. The institutions of marriage and the family are prime targets. Marriage is seen as domestic servitude, designed to ensure that men are fed and pampered, and have a steady supply of sex. Families are the training grounds of patriarchy, which produce the next generation of oppressors and victims—otherwise known as sons and daughters.

Critics of radical feminism point out that there is no need to deconstruct marriage and the family, since these institutions are breaking down on their own. In the fifties, a typical family consisted of a husband who worked nine-to-five and a wife who stayed at home to raise two or three children. Today, there seem to be no typical families left. Divorce, single motherhood, homosexual adoptions, lesbian couples and cohabitation have rewritten all the rules.

Yet radical feminists claim to see a common denominator: namely, the oppression of all female members. This is said to be true even of a family made up entirely of females. Why? Because their relationships are formed by external patriarchal pressures.

To radical feminists, the root of the problem lies in the male character, almost in male biology itself. In the watershed book *Against Our Will*, Susan Brownmiller traces the inevitability of rape back to Neanderthal times, when men began to use their penises as weapons. Brownmiller writes: "From prehistoric times to the present, I believe, rape has played a critical function. It is nothing more or less than a conscious process of intimidation by which *all men keep all women* in a state of fear."[6] (Emphasis in original.)

How she acquired this amazing knowledge of prehistoric sexual customs is not known.

Heterosexuality as gender oppression is a continuing theme of anti-pornography feminists. From Dworkin's book *Intercourse* (1987) to MacKinnon's statement "Heterosexuality . . . institutionalizes male sexual dominance and female sexual submission" in *Toward a Feminist Theory of the State* (1989),[7] one thing is clear: The male sex drive is a political yoke imposed on women.

Having established—to their satisfaction—the horrors of heterosexuality, radical feminists turn their intellectual guns on another aspect of patriarchy: capitalism. After all, pornography can almost be defined as commercialized sex. Their attack on capitalism lays the final groundwork for a full-out assault on porn. As Catharine MacKinnon observes in *Only Words*: "The sex is not chosen for the sex. Money is the medium of force and provides the cover of consent."[8]

Women's oppression is considered to stem from the twin evils of patriarchy and capitalism: sex and commercialism.

Armed with the battering ram of rage, radical feminists are making a frontal assault on the very symbol of heterosexuality and capitalism: pornography.

THE HISTORY OF THE ANTI-PORN FEMINIST CRUSADE

The seventies were the heydays of pornography, which flourished in an atmosphere of legal tolerance. In the early eighties, however, a parade of proposed legislation, based on radical feminist assumptions, aimed at suppressing pornography.

The first significant proposed legislation was the Minneapolis Anti-Pornography Ordinance. Andrea Dworkin and Catharine MacKinnon were hired as consultants by the conservative city legislators who wished to shut down the pornography shops.

Previous attempts to close the shops under zoning laws had failed. Dworkin and MacKinnon prepared an ordinance that redefined pornography as sex discrimination.

Drafted as a civil rights law, the ordinance would have given individual women, or groups of women, the right to take producers or distributors of pornography to civil court for damages. The charge would have been "coercing the plaintiff(s) into pornography"—that is, forcing a woman to participate in pornography without her consent.

The ordinance listed thirteen conditions which were not considered to be evidence of a woman's consent. Under the ordinance, a woman who had posed for pornographic pictures could have subsequently sued a magazine for publishing them even though she was of age, she had full knowledge of the purpose of the pictures, she signed a contract and a release, she was under no threat, there were witnesses to her cooperation, she showed no resistance, and she was fully paid. None of these factors were considered legal evidence of consent. In essence, the ordinance prohibited the possibility of consent.

Then, Dworkin and MacKinnon orchestrated the public hearings at which the ordinance was aired. They called only the witnesses they wished to hear from. Sex-abuse victims and social scientists gave long testimonies about the horrors of pornography. Civil rights advocates, gay activists, and the city attorney's office were excluded from the hearings. The ordinance passed with a speed that precluded any real examination of its implications. The mayor vetoed it.

The next target for an anti-pornography ordinance was Indianapolis. There, conservative anti-porn groups had been active, but not successful. The Republican mayor of Indianapolis, William Hudnut III, was also a Presbyterian minister. He saw the Minneapolis Ordinance as a prototype, and the perfect means to rid his city of pornography. Again, MacKinnon was hired as a consultant. Again, the ordinance passed.

Publishers and booksellers challenged the law in Federal District Court; they won. The case was appealed. In 1984, the court ruling *American Booksellers Association* v. *Hudnut*[9] overthrew the ordinance as unconstitutional. The court was particularly concerned about prohibiting such vaguely defined images as the "sexually explicit subordination of women"; indeed, the ordinance's descriptions were so vague as to constitute prior restraint. That is, pornographers and vendors would have to censor themselves for fear of crossing some unknown line. Attempts to introduce similar ordinances in Los Angeles, Suffolk County, Long Island, and both Cambridge and Brookline, Massachusetts, proved unsuccessful.

Recently, however, courts have begun to look more favorably on anti-pornography arguments. For example, in its 1991 ruling on *Barnes* v. *Glen Theatre, Inc.*[10] the U.S. Supreme Court held that nude dancing constitutes expression under the First Amendment and recognized that such dancing has been an important part of cultures throughout history. Nevertheless, the Supreme Court upheld a complete ban on nude dancing within a certain community, because the majority of that community found it morally offensive.

In February 1992, the Canadian Supreme Court embodied the MacKinnon/Dworkin perspective on pornography into law through its decision on *Butler* v. *Regina.*[11] It restricted the importation of material that "degrades" or "dehumanizes" women. The Court recognized pornography to be an aspect of free expression, but ruled that the prevention of harm to women was more important than freedom of speech.

Ironically, this obscenity law has been used almost exclusively against gay, lesbian, and feminist material.

Also in 1992, Senate Bill 1521—the Victims of Pornography Compensation Act—was being considered by the Senate Judiciary Committee. To its credit, one of the most influential voices against the censorship of pornography came from another faction within the feminist movement: liberal feminism. A news release from the liberal organization Feminists for Free Expression [FFE] described S.1521:

> The bill would have allowed crime victims to sue for unlimited money damages the producer, distributor, exhibitor and retailer of any book, magazine, movie or music that victims claim triggered the crime that harmed them. . . . It is because FFE is so concerned about violence that we protested this red-herring distraction from its causes. A rapist, under this bill, could leave court a free man while the owner of a local bookstore could not.[12]

Largely because of FFE's concerted and vocal opposition, S.1521 was dropped from the Senate agenda.

The criticism of liberal feminists has posed something of a dilemma for radical feminists. They have been able to contemptuously dismiss women who are sex workers, because these women have so little status within society that few people listen to them anyway. It is more difficult to ignore liberal feminists, many of whom have been prominent within the movement for years. When the pornography actress Marilyn Chambers defends pornography, she can be written off as a brainwashed victim who has fallen in love with her own oppression. When the President of the American Civil Liberties Union (ACLU), Nadine Strossen, argues against censorship in her book *Defending Pornography* (1995), a different line of dismissal must be taken.

Radical feminists disown their liberal counterparts and accuse them of working for the interests of patriarchy.

In the anthology *Sexual Liberals and the Attack on Feminism* (1990), editor Dorchen Leidholdt claims that feminists who believe women make their own choices about pornography are, in fact, spreading "a felicitous lie" (p. 131). Wendy Stock accuses free speech feminists of identifying with their oppressors "much like . . . concentration camp prisoners with their jailors" (p. 150). Valerie Heller proclaims that sexual liberals "create myths to disguise and distort the effect of exploitative, abusive behavior . . . placing the responsibility for the continued oppression of the victim on the victim herself" (p. 157). Andrea Dworkin accuses her feminist critics of running a "sex protection racket," and maintains that no one who defends pornography can be a feminist (p. 136).[13]

Liberal feminists who dare to speak up meet with abuse and dismissal. Anti-pornography feminists deal with the liberal threat of sexual tolerance by simply defining liberals out of the movement. That's one way to eliminate dissent.

If radical feminist attacks against pornography spill over onto liberal feminists or women in the industry, so be it. These women can be redefined as traitors or as "victims" who require saving, whether or not they want salvation.

Women who actively enjoy pornography, or who speak out for the rights of pornographers, are treated with special contempt. At a National Woman and the Law Conference in 1985, for example, Catharine MacKinnon debated Nan Hunter, of Feminists Against Censorship Taskforce. MacKinnon accused Hunter of being there "to speak for the pornographers, although that will not be what she says she is doing." She left no doubt that long-time activist Hunter was no longer a sister feminist.

Radical feminists have been distanced from their liberal counterparts. Ironically, however, they have become allied with another group of women: conservatives. Conservative women have been the *bête noire* of the feminist movement, because they oppose the full slate of feminist goals, from abortion to comparable worth. But these same women are willing to join hands with radical feminists on pornography. They are willing to march side-by-side in order to "take back the night." Why? Because they can co-opt the radical feminist agenda and use it for their own gains.

In Indianapolis, for example, the anti-pornography ordinance was backed by the religious right wing *and* the radical feminists. Local feminist groups gave it no support whatsoever. They spoke out against it. In Suffolk County, New York, the ordinance was put forward by an anti-ERA male legislator who claimed to be restoring to "ladies . . . what they used to be."

Radical feminists have not only allied with conservatives, they have also called for help from their arch enemy, the patriarchal state. They have asked the state to provide legislation to restrict sexual expression. They have asked the patriarchal state for protection. It is a bewildering sight to see radical feminists appealing to a system that they themselves condemn as irredeemably corrupt. Yet, in *Only Words*, MacKinnon applauds the court system, whenever she perceives an advantage in its rulings. It is to the state that radical feminists now appeal for protection against pornography. Do they truly believe that women, not men, will pass and enforce the laws that result?

Even more frightening: Some liberal feminists—feminists like Ellie Smeal, president of the Fund for a Feminist Majority —are pushing aside their free speech principles and campaigning for anti-pornography laws. In the March 12, 1993, issue of *The New York Times,* Smeal declared of pornography, "I am not going to just sit here and ignore it any longer. The violence toward women is there, everywhere. . . . I don't want a police state. . . . But to do nothing, to not enter out of fear is wrong. We have to get beyond, 'We can't do anything,' and do something."[14]

That "something" is the quick fix of censorship.

RADICAL FEMINISM'S SPECIFIC ACCUSATIONS AGAINST PORNOGRAPHY

Let's turn to the specific accusations being hurled at pornography. Porn is being attacked on three basic levels:

1. Pornography is morally wrong.
2. Pornography leads directly to violence against women.
3. Pornography, in and of itself, *is* violence against women. It is violence in several ways:
   a. Women are physically coerced into pornography;
   b. Women involved in the production of pornography who have not been physically coerced, have been so psychologically damaged by patriarchy that they are incapable of giving informed or "real" consent;
   c. Capitalism is a system of "economic coercion" that forces women into pornography in order to make a living;
   d. Pornography is violence against women who consume it, and thereby reinforce their own oppression; and,
   e. Pornography is violence against women, as a class, who must live in fear because of the atmosphere of terror it creates.

Do these accusations stand up under examination?

Pornography is morally wrong.

It is said that pornography is the way men subjugate women, in order to maintain their own position of power. It is the way men degrade and objectify women. Radical feminists avoid words like *good* or *evil.* They prefer to use more politically/sexually correct terms like *oppression* and *exploitation.*

Let's examine the second accusation first: the idea that pornography is degrading to women. *Degrading* is a subjective term. Personally, I find detergent commercials in which women become orgasmic over soapsuds to be tremendously degrading to women. I find movies in which prostitutes are treated like ignorant drug addicts to be slander against women. Every woman has the right—the need!—to define degradation for herself.

Next it is charged that pornography objectifies women: It converts them into sexual objects. Again, what does this mean? If taken literally, it means nothing at all because objects don't have sexuality; only human beings do. But the charge that pornography portrays women as "sexual beings" would not inspire rage and, so, it has no place in the anti-porn rhetoric.

Usually, the term *sex objects* means that women are shown as "body parts"; they are reduced to being physical objects. What is wrong with this? Women are as much their bodies as they are their minds or souls. No one gets upset if you present a women as a brain or as a spiritual being. Yet those portrayals ignore women as physical beings. To get upset by an image that focuses on the human body is merely to demonstrate a bad attitude toward what is physical. If I concentrated on a woman's sense of humor to the exclusion of her other characteristics, would this be degrading? Why is it degrading to focus on her sexuality? Underlying this attitude is the view that sex must be somehow ennobled to be proper.

And, for that matter, why is a naked female body more of an "object" than a clothed one?

Pornography, it is said, presents false images about women. Pornography is a lie, because it presents women as large-breasted nymphomanics. If this accusation is true, the remedy is not to ban pornography, but to recruit a wider variety of women into the industry.

Moreover, if accuracy is the hallmark of whether or not images should be banned, then much more than pornography should be censored. For example, women in the ads in *Working Woman* tend to be underweight, casually sophisticated, young business-women. Doesn't accuracy demand that they be a little over-weight, with a strand of hair out of place, perhaps even a bit frumpy? Do housewives feel degraded when they see the *Working Woman* caricature of a politically aware woman?

If society is to regulate depictions because they disturb some people, then we are reduced to the level of Andrea Dworkin, who castigates the painter Goya for exploiting women in his nude studies. Freedom means self-fulfillment. It also means putting up with other people's irritating pursuit of the same. It means being confronted by disturbing images and ideas.

Yet the charge lingers: Pornography is immoral. And, by some standard not my own, I'm sure it could be judged so. *I* find pornography to be morally acceptable and desirable, but I admit this is an open debate. The significant legal question, however, is, What does it matter? Why should the law concern itself with whether or not pornography is moral?

Underlying the anti-porn assault is an assumption regarding the purpose of law in society. And, since legal sanctions are being suggested, it is useful to examine this assumption.

There are two basic and fundamentally antagonistic views regarding the purpose of law in society. The first one, to which individualist feminists subscribe, is that the law should protect rights. It should protect self-ownership. "A woman's body, a woman's right" applies not only to abortion, but to every peaceful activity a woman engages in. The law should come into play only when a woman initiates force or has force initiated against her.

The second view of the purpose of law is shared by both conservatives and anti-porn feminists. It is that the law should protect virtue. Law should enforce proper moral behavior.

From this perspective, certain acts (or images or words) are wrong. They ought to be suppressed whether or not they constitute peaceful behavior. Classic examples are laws against blasphemy, pornography, and homosexuality. Because men should not regard women as "body parts," the law should discourage this tendency. By this standard, laws come into play whenever there has been a breach of public morality—read, breach of "women's class interests."

Liberal feminists have tried to bridge these two positions. They have tried to produce the best of both worlds by mixing a commitment to "a woman's body, a woman's right" with a demand for respecting women.

Their efforts are doomed, for one simple reason: the sticky issue of a woman's consent. What will liberal feminists say to women who choose to put themselves in situations where they are not respected—at least, by feminist standards? What will they say to the women who rush to pose for S/M pornography? To women who compete for the privilege?

If liberal feminists say that participation in pornography should be tolerated, they are conceding that the morality of it is irrelevant to whether it should be legal. If they say it should be prohibited, they are denying that a woman has a right to control her own body. A confrontation between these two views is inevitable. When you enforce virtue, you deny a woman's right to make an unacceptable choice with her own body.

This conflict is old wine in new bottles; it is nothing less than the age-old battle between freedom and control.

Pornography leads to violence against women.
The second basic accusation hurled against pornography is that it causes violence against women. Radical feminists claim there is a cause-and-effect relationship between men viewing pornography and men attacking women, especially in the form of rape.

But studies and experts disagree as to whether there is any

relationship between pornography and violence. Or, more broadly stated, between images and behavior. Even the procensorship Meese Commission Report admitted that much of the data connecting pornography to violence was unreliable.

This Commission was the last national effort to define and suppress pornography. It was a circus of public hearings, conducted by the U.S. Attorney General's Commission on Pornography aka the Meese Commission. Established in May 1984, this eleven-person body received a mandate from President Ronald Reagan to investigate what he called "new evidence linking pornography to anti-social behavior." Reagan obviously wanted to overturn the findings of the 1970 Federal Commission on Pornography and Obscenity, which had been set up by thenpresident Richard Nixon. The earlier commission not only found no link between violence and pornography, it also urged the repeal of most obscenity laws. Its findings were dismissed.

The Meese Commission carefully avoided a repetition of this embarrassing liberalism. For example, the first Meese hearing allowed testimony from forty-two anti-porn advocates as opposed and only three pro-freedom of speech people. Many anticensorship groups, including major writers' organizations, were denied the chance to speak. The reason given: lack of time.

But when radical feminist Dorchen Leidholt, who had already testified, rushed the microphone along with a group of other women, she was given extra time. The microphones stayed switched on. And a written copy of her remarks were requested by the chairman.

Is it any wonder that the Meese Commission found there to be a relationship between pornography and violence? In the *Virginia Law Review*, Nadine Strossen commented on the shaky ground beneath this finding: "The Meese Commission . . . relied on Professor Murray Straus' correlational studies . . . to 'justify' their conclusions that exposure to 'pornography' leads to sexual assaults. But, as Professor Straus wrote the Commission, 'I do not believe that [my] research demonstrates that pornography causes rape.' "[15]

Other studies, such as the one prepared by feminist Thelma McCormick (1983) for the Metropolitan Toronto Task Force on Violence Against Women, found no pattern to indicate a connection between pornography and sex crimes. Incredibly, the Task Force suppressed the study and re-assigned the project to a pro-censorship male, who returned the "correct" results. His study was published.

Moving away from studies, what of real world feedback? In West Germany, rape rates have slightly declined since 1973, when pornography became widely available; meanwhile, other violent crime has increased. In Japan, where pornography depicting violence is widely available, rape is much lower per capita than in the United States, where violence in porn is restricted.

It can be argued that all forms of violence are lower in these countries. The low rate of violence against women may be nothing more than a reflection of this. Nevertheless, if pornography *is* intimately connected to violence against women, you would expect to see that connection to be manifested in some manner. It is up to radical feminists to explain why it is not.

But even generously granting the assumption that a correlation *does* exist between pornography and violence, what would such a correlation tell us? It would certainly not indicate a cause-and-effect relationship. It is a fallacy to assume that if A can be correlated with B, then A causes B. Such a correlation may indicate nothing more than that both are caused by another factor, C. For example, there is a high correlation between the number of doctors in a city and the number of alcoholics there. One doesn't cause the other; both statistics are proportional to the size of the city's population.

Those researchers who draw a relationship between pornography and violence tend to hold one of two contradictory views on what that connection might be. The first view is that porn is a form of catharsis. That is, the more pornography we see, the less likely we are to act out our sexual urges. The second view is that porn inspires imitation. That is, the more pornography we see, the more likely we are to imitate the sexual behavior it represents.

Researchers who favor the catharsis theory point to studies, such as the one conducted by Berl Kutchinsky, which found that an increased availability of pornography in Denmark correlated with a decrease in the sex offenses committed there.

Radical feminists advocate the imitation theory, the idea that men will try to recreate the situations they see on a screen. The first comment to make about this claim is how insulting it is to men. Radical feminists seem to believe that men are soulless lumps of plasticine on which pornographers can leave any imprint they wish.

Although anti-porn feminists cry out against viewing pornography, they must admit that there is at least one group of people who can survive such exposure without harm—namely, themselves. In their zeal, radical feminists view more pornography than the general population. Moreover, they dwell upon the small percentage of pornography that depicts violence. Either they are wonder women or they are human beings who have a normal response to brutal pornography: They are repelled by it.

Radical feminists are well aware of how disturbing most people find brutal pornography. This is precisely the reaction they count on when they show pornographic slides and films at lectures and debates. They count on the fact that most people are revolted by graphic violence and brutality. Ironically, this revulsion has sometimes worked against the anti-porn cause. Several years ago in New York City, the group Feminists Fighting Pornography was ordered to remove a display of pornography that it had set up in Grand Central Terminal. Commuters were upset by the sight of it. The New York Civil Liberties Union successfully defended the feminists' right to display pornography.

Despite the evidence that most people are repelled by pornography that depicts violence, radical feminists parade anecdotal studies that draw the connections they desire. For example, interviews in which rapists confess they consumed violent pornography before committing their crime. Even if these stories are credible, they indicate nothing more than that men who rape may also tend to enjoy brutal images of sex. They say nothing about the reactions of men in general.

There is no reason to believe that pornography causes violence. There is a growing body of evidence that indicates that pornography either acts as a catharsis or has little impact at all.

Pornography is *violence against women.*
The third accusation anti-porn feminists hurl is that pornography, in and of itself, is an act of violence. It is violence committed against every woman, whether or not she is personally exposed to it.

The type of violence done to the woman changes, however, depending on her relationship to pornography. The most direct harm is said to be inflicted on the women most directly involved. Women who participate in the production of pornography are said to be victimized in one of several ways: They are physically coerced into pornography; they are so psychologically damaged that they are rendered incapable of giving informed or "real" consent; they have been forced by capitalism to sell their bodies for the camera.

Women outside the industry are also considered to be victims because if they consume it, they reinforce their own oppression; and, even if they do not consume it, they must live in the atmosphere of terror that pornography creates throughout society.

Let's consider these accusations one by one:

Women are physically coerced into pornography.
My research indicates the contrary. But I would never deny the possibility that coercion exists. Every industry has its abuses.

Nevertheless, the claim of "coercion into pornography" generally rests on a few horrifying and well-publicized accounts by women who had worked in the industry. After leaving, they claimed they had been coerced into performing pornographic acts. These accounts must not be cavalierly dismissed.

Nor should they be given a rubber stamp of acceptance. If the specific charges are found to be true, this truth should not be allowed to drown out the voices of women who have benefited from pornography.

If a specific charge of "coercion into pornography" is proven true, those who used force or threats to make a woman perform should be charged with kidnapping, assault, and/or rape. Any pictures or films that result from the coercion should be confiscated and burned, because no one has the right to benefit from the proceeds of a crime.

What radical feminists propose, however, offers women less protection than they already have. Radical feminists insist that "coercion into pornography" is a civil rights violation, a form of discrimination against women. According to them, a man who kidnaps a woman, imprisons her, and forces her to pose at gunpoint has not committed a criminal act, but a civil one. Instead, feminists should be calling for the full enforcement of criminal laws.

Women in porn who have not been physically coerced have been so traumatized by patriarchy that they cannot give "real" consent. And the absence of real consent is the equivalent of coercion.

This is the second way in which women in the industry are said to be victims of violence. They are said to be so brainwashed by white male culture that they cannot render consent. Thus, they are *de facto* coerced.

Consider how arrogant this statement is.

Although women in pornography *appear* to be willing, anti-porn feminists see through this charade. They know that no psychologically healthy woman would agree to the humiliation and degradation of pornography. If agreement seems to be present, it is only because the women have been so emotionally beaten down they have fallen in love with their own oppression. In order to restore real choice to these victims, feminists must rescue them from themselves. In other words, any woman who poses for pornography is psychologically damaged, by definition, and her avowed wishes need not be respected. Like a mentally ill patient, she is incapable of acting in her own interests because she is incapable of knowing what they are.

If a woman enjoys performing sex acts in front of a camera, it is not because she is a unique human being who reasons and reacts from a different background or personality. No. It is because she is psychologically damaged and no longer responsible for her actions. She must, in effect, become a political ward of radical feminists, who will make the correct choices for her.

This is more than an attack on the right to pose for pornography. It is a denial of a woman's right to choose anything outside the narrow corridor of choices offered by political/sexual correctness.

The right to choose hinges on the right to make a "wrong" choice. Freedom of religion entails the right to be an atheist. Freedom of speech involves the right to be silent. Freedom of choice requires the right to make bad choices—that is, a decision society considers to be wrong. After all, society is not going to stop a woman from doing what it wants her to do.

But radical feminists are going one step farther than simply denying that women have the right to make wrong choices; they deny that women have the *ability* to choose.

How do radical feminists explain away the abundant and clear evidence of consent—contracts, witnesses, personal testimony, releases, etc.—provided by these women? They handle this sticky issue by redefining consent so as to make it unrecognizable. According to the Minneapolis ordinance drafted by Mac-Kinnon and Dworkin, for example, the following factors do not indicate the presence of consent: that the woman is of age; that she showed no resistance; that a contract was signed and witnessed; that payment was received.

According to radical feminists, even if a woman in pornography signed a contract with full knowledge, she can sue on the grounds of coercion. What legal implications does this have for a woman's right to contract? What legal weight will future negotiators give to a woman's signature? Women's contracts will be legally unenforceable; their signature will become a legal triviality.

For centuries, women have struggled against tremendous odds to have their contracts taken seriously. At great personal expense, they stood up and demanded the right to own land, to control their own wages, to retain custody of their children—in other words, to become legally responsible for themselves and for their property. A woman's consent must never again become legally irrelevant.

Yet this is what radical feminists propose to do. They claim that women are so weak-willed and feeble-minded that cultural pressures easily overwhelm their free will and make them into the play things of patriarchy.

Consider one fact: *Everyone* is formed by their culture. The very language with which we speak and formulate thought comes from our culture. And certainly there are times when cultural pressures lead people to make bad choices. But to say that any woman who poses nude does so only because she has been indoctrinated by patriarchy, is to eliminate the possibility of her ever choosing anything.

In other words, if one choice is invalidated because of cultural influences, all choices are invalidated. Why? Because *all* choices are culturally influenced if only because the people making them have been shaped by experience. Every decision is made in the presence of cultural pressures. To invalidate a woman's choices is to deny her the one protection she has against an unhealthy culture: namely, the right to decide for herself.

Yet this is what radical feminists propose. And they do so under the guise of protecting psychologically damaged women.

Pause for a moment. Think of what is being said.

Anti-porn feminists want us to accept their sexual preferences as gospel. Presumably, their theories are based on solid fact and deep insight. Although they have been born and raised in the same patriarchal culture which has warped other women, radical feminists have somehow escaped unscathed. Just as they have escaped being damaged by the pornography they view. Somehow these women have scaled the pinnacle, from which they now look down and make pronouncements on the lifestyle of those beneath them.

Perhaps radical feminists are superwomen. Perhaps they are merely fanatics unwilling to respect any position other than their own.

If women's choices are to be trashed, why should radical feminists fare better than other women? Are they the elite? If the choices of pornographic models are not to be taken seriously, radical feminists cannot claim respect for their choices either. If culture negates the free will of women, anti-porn feminists are in the same boat as the rest of us.

Capitalism is a system of "economic coercion" that forces women into pornography in order to make a living.

This is part and parcel of the accusation that pornography exploits women. Exploitation means getting something from someone in a manner that is hurtful, deceptive, or otherwise unfair.

This charge arises because pornography is a commercial activity. The anti-porn argument runs: Because in general women are paid less than men and have fewer opportunities, they are forced to enter unsavory professions in order to make a living.

Radical feminists such as Catharine MacKinnon, who calls herself a "post-Marxist," erase the line most people draw between a voluntary exchange and a forced one: This is the line between consent and coercion. They reject a woman's right to contract.

Contracts are records of voluntary exchanges. Labor contracts are voluntary exchanges of work for wages. Most people enter labor contracts—that is, get a job—because they need money. But, to radical feminists, this is "economic coercion." Because they believe the free market *forces* people to take jobs, they view it as a form of violence.

When radical feminists deny the validity of porn contracts, they are not attacking pornography, so much as they are attacking contracts themselves. If they reject porn contracts because the woman needs money, then they are logically constrained to reject almost every other labor contract as well.

A question should be asked: Do anti-porn feminists see any difference between offering a woman money for her services and putting a gun to her head to obtain the same thing? Politically, their theory claims there is no difference.

People's alternatives are always limited. This is not an indictment of the free market. It is a statement about reality and human nature. Consent is the application of free will to whatever choices are possible to you at a given moment. One of those choices is pornography.

Anti-porn feminists refuse to acknowledge the free will of women who make this choice. Instead, they construct an elaborate theory to explain how the women have been exploited by capitalism.

Only by understanding the deep and unmovable antipathy that radical feminists harbor toward free exchange and traditional sex is it possible to sound the near bottomless depths of their hatred for pornography, which combines both.

Pornography is violence against women who consume it, and thereby re-enforce their own oppression.

It is true that pornography repels many women; and this is an excellent reason for those women to avoid it. For others, however, pornography offers a wide range of pleasurable fantasies including: sex with a stranger, sex for the fun of it, with another woman, as a dominatrix, with a group, or with someone who is otherwise inaccessible. The majority of women lead conventional monogamous lives. Pornography allows them to vicariously enjoy a cornucopia of sex, without having to bear the consequences of actually doing anything.

But what of pornography that depicts mock violence? Doesn't sadomasochism express and promote the subjugation of women?

In her essay "The Art of Discipline," Susan Farr explains that the show of violence in sadomasochism cannot be judged by conventional standards. The behavior signifies something entirely different to those involved in it than it does to those on the outside. Farr explains that there is no one correct interpretation of the slaps and posturing that characterizes this form of sex play.

It is a purely personal response. And the personal is not political.

Pornography is violence against women, as a class, who must live in fear because of the atmosphere of terror it creates.

An assumption underlies this claim: namely, that women are not individuals, but members of a class with collective interests.

Radical feminists claim to have discovered the correct collective class will of women. They have uncovered the sexually correct choice that every woman should make. They have also revealed the enemy: men as a class.

If men object to being lumped together as oppressors, they are ignored. They are seen as simply defending *their* collective class interests. If individual women object to being denied access to pornography, they are ignored. Obviously, such women have been psychologically damaged by patriarchy and no longer know their own minds. They no longer perceive their own class interest.

To radical feminists, individual freedom creates a natural disharmony of interests among women. After all, if a woman can make her own sexual choice without infringing on the equal right of another woman to choose, then there are no collective interests —just individuals peacefully pursuing their own visions. Such a possibility would destroy the structure of class rights.

To condemn pornography, radical feminists must condemn the concept of individuality. They must deny that personal choices are personal.

This is the message behind phrases like the "collective rights" and "the class interests" of woman: The choices of individuals must be subordinated. The correct class choice must be enforced. And this correct choice can be discerned only by the politically enlightened, the politically elite. The arrogance of this attitude is astounding.

Denying sexual choice to women is an accusation commonly hurled at patriarchy. Now radical feminists are doing the same thing. They clothe their actions by claiming that wrong decisions are not real ones, but merely the reflection of patriarchy.

What is really being reflected is anti-porn feminism's contempt for anyone—even women—who disagree.

SELF-CONTRADICTIONS WITHIN ANTI-PORN FEMINISM

As vigorously as radical feminists attack pro-sex arguments, they seem strangely blind to flaws in their own position. It is difficult to imagine how any woman with intellectual honesty could miss the contradictions and inconsistencies of the anti-porn position. These contradictions include:

• Radical feminists claim that pornography is a civil rights violation, and therefore not protected under the First Amendment. It is not political or social speech; it is an abuse of speech. Yet they also argue that pornography is one of the main expressions of patriarchy, which is a political system. The more they rail against pornography as a prop of patriarchy, the more it resembles precisely the type of political expression meant to be protected by the First Amendment.

• Radical feminists are committed to "validating" the experiences of women who have been silenced by patriarchy. They are determined to rediscover women's history, or "herstory," through which the voices of real women will finally be heard. Yet they vigorously dismiss the voices of women who choose to participate in pornography.

• Pornography is said to be a bastion of patriarchy and, thus, the enemy of women's rights. Conservatives, who are said to support patriarchy, also oppose women's rights. If both statements are true, why do conservatives crusade against pornography?

On the other hand, pornography is anti-family in that it breaks the traditional ties between sex and motherhood, sex and marriage. Since radical feminists consider the family to be a building block of patriarchy, why aren't they pleased to see it under attack? How can pornography attack family values *and* support patriarchy at the same time?

• Anti-porn feminism touts the natural power of women, but it seems to have political interest in women as "victims." Even powerful women, like porn producer Candida Royalle, who is also on the board of Feminists for Free Expression, are seen as pathetic pawns of men. Which is true: Are women powerful beings or are they natural victims?

• Censorship is used by those who have power against those who do not. By radical feminists' own standards, censorship will be used by men who control the state against women who do not. If the patriarchal state is *the* problem, how can it intervene on women's behalf?

Nevertheless, radical feminists *must* use the state. They wish to force their code of conduct on others. They do not wish to persuade or educate, because it is unlikely that either of these peaceful tactics would completely eliminate pornography. Only force can do this. Only the state can provide it.

• If pornography disappeared tomorrow, our culture would still be flooded with images of women that many would consider degrading and humiliating. To be consistent, radical feminists have to call for banning sexually incorrect TV, literature, art, and advertising. The fact that they have been fairly quiet on this point may well be a matter of strategy. Pornography is an easy target compared to the evening news.

• Radical feminists draw a distinction between pornography (which is anti-woman) and erotica (which is pro-woman). They glowingly describe what constitutes erotica. Yet, by their own standards, they can have no idea of what erotica would look like. By their own admission, it would be created by a postcapitalist, postpatriarchal society, which does not exist. Nor can they claim to know what women will want sexually once patriarchy has been swept away. Of course, this does not prevent radical feminists from describing in detail how women would sexually react without patriarchy. They seem to have a vision of the future that is denied to the rest of us.

CRITIQUE OF ANTI-PORNOGRAPHY RESEARCH
The methodology of the anti-pornography crusaders is as flawed as their ideology. Theories are paraded as fact. Ad hominem at-

tacks take the place of arguments. Instead of blind studies or hard statistics, anti-porn feminists give broad overview of how women have been portrayed in literature and art. Objectivity is either openly scorned as a "male characteristic" or simply ignored.

For example, the huge tome entitled *Sourcebook on Pornography* purports to give a balanced overview of the issue, complete with chapters on "civil libertarians" and other advocates of sexual freedom. Nevertheless, Chapter One opens: "Pornography is an $8 billion a year business that legitimizes and encourages rape, torture, and degradation of women. It is created by filming real or simulated sexually explicit acts of sexual torture, abuse, degradation or terrorism against real people."[16]

Radical feminism is an ideology in search of supporting facts. And to their credit, anti-pornography feminists usually make no pretense of fairness.

An example of their open prejudice occurred at a purportedly "unbiased" conference on prostitution held in fall 1992 at the University of Michigan Law School, where Catharine MacKinnon teaches. All of the conference speakers opposed legalizing prostitution. Nevertheless, the students who had organized the conference set up an exhibit which presented a range of views on prostitution—some favorable. The students were forced to dismantle the exhibit. Dissenting views—even on the sidelines, even from the feminist organizers of the conference—were not to be permitted.

From the large pool of research and perspectives, radical feminists draw only upon those sources which support their conclusions. They are fond of validating the Reagan-sponsored Meese Commission Report, while totally ignoring the 1970 Presidential Commission on Pornography assembled by Nixon to condemn porn. This despite the fact that the 1970 Commission was far more thorough than the Meese Commission.

The 1970 Commission funded a survey of 2,486 adults and 769

young people to determine the extent to which pornography was damaging them. To the question, Would you please tell me what you think are the two or three most serious problems facing the country today? only two percent of respondents expressed a concern over pornography. Twenty-four percent said porn gave them "information about sex." Ten percent said it improved their sexual relations. Those who reported recent exposure to pornography tended to report positive effects. Moreover, the vast majority of experts consulted did not draw a connection between pornography and social harm.

The 1970 Commission also studied crime rates. It found that although sexual material became seven times more available between 1960 to 1969, sexual crimes by juveniles decreased during that period. Nevertheless—perhaps sensitive to the fact that their official *raison d'être* was to condemn porn—the Commission backed away from saying there was no connection between pornography and violence. It stated instead:

> Research to date thus provides no substantial basis for the belief that erotic materials constitute a primary or significant cause of the development of character deficits or that they operate as a significant determinative factor in causing crime and delinquency. This conclusion is stated with due and perhaps excessive caution, since it is obviously not possible, and never would be possible, to state that never on any occasion, under any condition, did any erotic material ever contribute in any way to the likelihood of any individual committing a sex crime. Indeed, no such statement could be made about any kind of nonerotic material. On the basis of the available data, however, it is not possible to conclude that erotic material is a significant cause of crime.[17]

This vindication of pornography led then President Richard Nixon to declare, "So long as I am in the White House, there will be no relaxation of the national effort to control and eliminate smut from our national life. . . . I totally reject this report."[18]

Radical feminists agree with Nixon.

The growing intolerance within feminism is not a sign of intellectual confidence, which invites open discussion. It is a sign of dogmatic hostility toward anyone who disagrees. It is coupled with bad science and poor research.

In general, most studies of pornography follow one of two methodologies, both of which try to draw connections between images and behavior:

1. They expose men to pornographic material in a lab setting and observe the immediate effects; or
2. They try to correlate what men report reading or watching with the behavior of those men.

The first type of research has many possible shortcomings. Any one of them could invalidate its findings. The possible shortcomings include: The lab study may not reflect behavior in the real world; the subject or the researcher might introduce unknown factors (e.g., the emotional response of the researcher); the subjects—often criminals or students—may not be representative of the general population, or even representative of most criminals or students; the artificial situation in and of itself may induce aggression (e.g., no punishment is attached to behavior); the pornography viewed is selective; the impact of pornography is short-lived and easily overridden by the next stimulus; most studies rely on immediate responses and do not indicate what behavior, if any, would follow in the real world; the extent to which pornography causes harm by, for example, changing morality, is impossible to scientifically measure.

The second research methodology suffers from similar pitfalls.

Added to this is the credibility problem of having to believe whatever the subject says. This is a particularly sticky problem when the subjects are rapists who wish to blame their crime on some external force.

Moreover, the researcher typically brings assumptions to the experiment, which shape the results. This is true of the most scrupulously honest study. For example, if a researcher believes that sex is biologically based rather than a social construct, this assumption will influence what questions are asked and how the data is interpreted.

Whichever method is used, many researchers are openly skeptical that the results prove anything.

Research on the possible connection between images and actions, pornography and violence, is in its infancy. Anti-porn feminism is not allowing it to mature. Political/sexual correctness is the single greatest force blocking real investigation into violence against women.

Consider the issue of rape. In the sixties, researchers approached rape as a complex crime that had as many motives as any other violent act did. Consider murder: People murder for money, out of passion, as a part of war, for the thrill, out of jealousy, from peer pressure, for revenge, because they are on drugs or drunk . . . The list goes on. The Kinsey study classified no less than seven types of rapists.

Rape used to be considered in such complex, sophisticated terms. Today, political correctness—especially on the campus—has narrowed the range of permissible research that can be conducted. Rape now has only one cause: patriarchy. It is an act of power committed by men against women.

When political interests become mixed with methodology, reports and studies become virtually worthless.

So does analysis.

FIVE

LIBERAL FEMINISM: THE GLIMMER OF HOPE

In the maelstrom of anti-pornography hysteria, liberal feminism often provides the few voices of sanity heard above the storm. Liberal organizations like Feminists for Free Expression (FFE) have consistently and courageously stood up against measures like the Victims of Pornography Compensation Act, and for sexual expression. Some liberal feminists like Nadine Strossen have been staunch and tireless in their defense of freedom of speech. It is difficult to imagine better companions in the fight for sexual choice.

Other liberals seem to have forgotten their roots and are now willing to sacrifice free speech for the greater good of protecting women from pornography.

There is a growing schism within liberal feminism, which threatens to disrupt such key liberal organizations as the National Organization for Women (NOW) and the American Civil Liberties Union (ACLU).

What are the arguments that are causing such turmoil in liberal ranks?

LIBERAL FEMINIST ARGUMENTS AGAINST CENSORSHIP

In general, liberal feminists offer three types of arguments against censoring pornography: Freedom of speech is a necessary condition for human freedom; the suppression of pornography will hurt women (in the several ways presented below); and, pornography offers certain benefits to women.

Let us examine the first two arguments. The third will be discussed in the following chapter.

Freedom of speech is a necessary condition for human freedom.
This argument says little about women's relationship to pornography, except in the most general sense. Even feminists who believe porn degrades and humiliates women sometimes argue against censorship as the greater threat. These are the feminists who say: As a woman I am appalled by *Playboy*... but as a writer I understand the need for free speech.

Such feminists are not pro-pornography. They are anticensorship. They argue on several grounds: Great works of art and literature would be banned; the First Amendment would be breached; political expression would be suppressed; and a creative culture requires freedom of speech.

The suppression of pornography will hurt women.
This argument specifically addresses the relationship of women to pornography. But, again, it is not so much a defense of pornography as it is an attack on censorship. Liberal feminists point to the real problems involved in implementing the antipornography program. Among the insightful questions they ask are:

Who Will Act as Censor?

Whoever acts as censor will wield tremendous power, because words such as *degrading* are so subjective they will be interpreted to mean whatever the censor wants them to. In the August 1993 *Virginia Law Review*, Nadine Strossen worries that the anti-pornography definitions are so vague that they could be used against homosexual and lesbian material:

"It is not clear whether Andrea Dworkin or Catharine Mac-Kinnon would classify homoerotic photographs or films as 'pornography.' Although their model law defines 'pornography' as the 'sexually explicit subordination of *women* through pictures and/or words,' it expressly stipulates that even images of men could be interpreted as portraying the subordination of women."[1]

The state that banned Margaret Sanger because she used the words *syphilis* and *gonorrhea* is no different, in principle, than the one that interprets obscenity today.

There will be nothing—not even the paper shield of the First Amendment—to stand between the state and feminist literature. There will be no protection even for the feminist classics such as *Our Bodies, Ourselves,* which provided a generation of women with a explicit glimpse of their own sexuality.

Inevitably, censorship will be used against the least popular views, against the weakest members of society—including feminists and lesbians. When the Canadian Supreme Court decided (1992) to protect women by restricting the importation of pornography, one of the first targets was a lesbian/gay bookstore named Glad Day Bookstore, which had been on a police "hit list." Canadian officials also targeted university and radical bookstores. Among the books seized by Canadian customs were two books by Andrea Dworkin: *Pornography: Men Possessing Women* and *Women Hating.*

Even narrowing the definition of pornography to include only the depiction of explicit violence would not protect feminist works. It would not, for example, protect Susan Brownmiller's pivotal *Against Our Will,* which offers a "history" of rape, complete with graphic detail. Nor would it exempt Kate Millett's *The Basement*, a novel-chronicle of sexual torture.

Doesn't the Anti-Pornography Crusade Perpetuate the Myth of Women as Victims?

Refusing to acknowledge the contracts of women in pornography places them in the same legal category as children or mental incompetents. In Indianapolis, the anti-pornography ordinance argued that women, like children, needed special protection under the law:

"Children are incapable of consenting to engage in pornographic conduct.... By the same token, the physical and psychological well-being of women ought to be afforded comparable protection, for the coercive environment ... vitiates any notion that they consent or 'choose' to perform in pornography."[2]

This attitude of "I'm a helpless victim" could easily backfire on women who may be required to prove they are able to manage their own finances, or to handle custody of their own children. Moreover, the idea of men "emotionally or verbally coercing" women re-enforces the concept of men as intellectually and psychologically stronger than women. It is the old "Man of Steel/ Woman of Kleenex" myth.

Who Will Protect Women from the Anti-Feminist Conservatives, with Whom Radical Feminists Are Aligning?

By joining hands with conservatives, anti-pornography feminists have strengthened the political power of the Religious Right, who attack abortion and other fundamental rights of women. Radical feminists are being used. For example, in 1992, the promotional material of the conservative National Coalition Against Pornography featured quotes from Andrea Dworkin; in other contexts, these same people crucify her as a lesbian.

This alliance may be a tragic mistake for women's rights. With tragic results. Feminists are lending credibility and power to organizations which will turn on a dime against them.

Aren't Radical Feminists Diverting Attention from the Real Issues that Confront Women?

Feminists used to address the complex network of cultural, political, and biological factors that contributed to the real issues confronting women. Now the beginning and ending of all discussion seems to be the specter of patriarchy—of white male culture in league with capitalism. Pornography is merely one aspect of this single-minded assault. Radical feminist analysis is imposed on all forms of women's sexuality, including childbirth.

Consider the furor that is brewing around the New Reproductive Technologies (NRTs), which have been called "the pornography of pregnancy." These technologies—which include *in vitro* fertilization, surrogate motherhood, and embryo transfer—are behind the recent news stories announcing that sixty-year-old women are giving birth. Men have always been able to become parents at sixty; that door has just opened for women.

The NRTs raise many questions of medical and genetic ethics, including: how to redefine the family, what of population control; and what of world hunger. For radical feminists, however, there is but one issue. Medical science and technology are the products of white male culture, which oppresses women; therefore, the NRTs are medicalized terror conducted against women.

(Interestingly enough, the women who clamor for such medical procedures are dismissed in the same manner as women in pornography: namely, they are said to be brainwashed and no longer capable of true consent.)

Patriarchy seems to be blamed for everything from sexual harassment to stretch marks. It is a common saying: When all you have is a hammer, everything looks like a nail. When your ideology sounds only one note, all songs are in the same key.

Increasingly, violence against women seems to be linked—

almost attributed—to one source: pornography. This is not an opening up of feminist theory and consciousness; it is a closing down.

Doesn't Blaming Pornography Exonerate Rapists?

To blame words or images for the actions of people is simplistic. It retards any real examination into what motivates violent crimes, such as rape. Radical feminists are handing a "pornography made me do it" excuse to rapists. Nothing should be allowed to mitigate the personal responsibility of every man who physically abuses a woman.

Radical feminists are allowing men to introduce "extenuating circumstances" into their defense. For example, in appealing *Schiro* v. *Clark*,[3] the defendant—a rapist—argued that in sentencing, the judge had failed to take into account his consumption of "rape" pornography. Fortunately, his argument fell deservedly flat.

How Can Women Chronicle Their Oppression If They Do Not Have Access to Its History?

Censorship removes the evidence of women's oppression and limits their ability to learn from it. For example, if it had been up to Comstock and his nineteenth-century censorship drive, no evidence of the fledgling birth control movement would have survived. The record of this struggle survives only because individuals preserved periodicals and pamphlets, which were archived decades later by universities and historical societies.

How much lesbian history will be available if censorship prevails?

THE FLAW IN LIBERAL FEMINIST ARGUMENTS

Those liberals who defend pornography do not generally address the ideological underpinnings of the onslaught against it. They continue to view anti-porn feminists as fellow travelers, instead of seeing them as dangerous companions.

One reason for this is that liberal feminists share many of the ideological assumptions underlying the radical feminist attack. For example, both liberal and radical feminists condemn the free market for making a profit by using women as "body parts." Both believe that the commercialization of sex demeans women. In an essay meant to defend the rights of pornographers, Lisa Steel comments: "Sexist representation of women . . . is all part of the same system that, in the service of profits, reduces society to 'consumer groups.' And marketing is every bit as conservative as the military . . . we pay dearly for the 'rights' of a few to make profits from the rest of us."[4]

Is this a defense or an attack?

Liberal feminists also tend to use the radical feminist definition of pornography—a definition tremendously slanted in favor of censorship. Once women accept the anti-pornography definition, it is difficult to arrive at any position other than censorship. The Canadian sociologist Jill Ridington argues for free speech. Nevertheless, she defines pornography as: ". . . a presentation . . . of sexual behavior in which one or more participants are coerced, overtly or *implicitly*, into participation; or are injured or abused physically or *psychologically*; or in which an *imbalance of power* is obvious, or *implied* . . . and in which such behavior can be taken to be advocated or endorsed." (Emphasis added.)[5]

By this definition, what isn't pornography? What can't be interpreted as an imbalance of power? Since almost every sexual presentation is capable of causing psychological harm to someone, almost every presentation can be considered pornographic.

Pornography needs stauncher advocates.

Fortunately, it has them.

S I X

Individualist Feminism: A True Defense of Pornography

Individualist feminism provides the best defense of pornography because its ideology is the mirror image of radical feminism, from which the most effective attack on porn is coming. Individual feminism insists on the principle of self-ownership: a woman's body, a woman's right. It insists that women be free to choose, regardless of the content of their choices.

The key concept here is *choice*, which is present whenever a woman acts without physical coercion. Certainly, it is present whenever the woman herself says the actions are voluntary, because she is the only person truly capable of judging that claim. The peaceful choices of every woman must be respected; the voice of every woman should be heard.

This is a profoundly individualistic approach, which leaves little room for class analysis as presented by anti-porn feminists. Such feminists view individual rights and personal preferences as irritating bumps on the road to the greater good of class interest. To them, "the personal is political."

To individualist feminists, the personal is personal. There is a political door that closes to separate and protect individuals from society. People call this protection by different names: the Bill of Rights, self-ownership, individual rights, or natural law. In the shadow of this protection, individual women make decisions about matters that concern them and them alone. For example, they decide about sex.

This is not to say that one woman's sexual choices cannot have implications for another woman, or an impact upon her. Every action you take and every word you utter can impact upon another human being. Exhaling can have an impact, especially if you have a cold or some other contagious disease. The question is: At what point does another woman have a right to restrict your actions on the grounds of self-protection?

Individualist feminism answers: When, and only when, those actions involve physical force, threat of force, or fraud. In the absence of force, women should be free to make any and every sexual choice they wish.

I may not personally approve of their choices. I may find their choices distasteful. Nevertheless, every choice a woman makes enriches me, because it expands my range of alternatives—even if it is an alternative I can't imagine ever persuing myself.

The nineteenth-century individualist feminist Lillian Harman made a similar point:

> I consider uniformity in mode of sexual relations as undesirable and impractical as enforced uniformity in anything else. For myself, I want to profit by my mistakes . . . and why should I be unwilling for others to enjoy the same liberty? If I should be able to bring the entire world to live exactly as I live at present, what would that avail me in ten years, when as I hope, I shall have a broader knowledge of life, and my life therefore probably changed.[1]

To repeat: the key is choice. With regard to pornography, this means: Let individual women decide for themselves. Let them weigh the evidence and come to their own conclusions.

But what of the women who are upset by the mere fact that pornography exists? Aren't they "forced" to live in a pornographic world? In a word, yes. Women who like pornography force others to live in a pornographic world in the same manner that women who lack taste in clothes force others to live with their fashion sense. *Every* peaceful act can affect someone else. Again, the question is: Do the effects deny to anyone what they have the right to demand?

The answer is no. My decision to consume pornography in no way infringes on another woman's ability to walk right past it. She can express her disapproval—through speaking out, picketing, and boycott. What she must not do is introduce the force of law.

The mere fact that some women are upset by the presence of pornography tells us very little. It tells us nothing about whether porn is right or wrong, valuable or useless. After all, feminism distresses a great many people. Yet feminists would argue that the movement should not only be tolerated, it should be nurtured. They consider women's rights to have a positive, rather than a negative effect on society—even if it causes distress. Perhaps the same is true of the graphic depiction of sex.

This is the position I maintain. I argue that the benefits pornography provides to women far outweigh any of its disadvantages. But, at its root, the argument for pornography is not utilitarian.

Pornography should be defended out of respect for women's choices and for human sexual diversity.

AN INDIVIDUALIST FEMINIST DEFENSE OF PORNOGRAPHY

Pornography and feminism have many things in common. They both focus on women as sexual beings. Pornography dwells on the physical act of sex itself; feminism examines the impact of sex upon women—historically, economically, politically, and culturally.

Pornography is one of the windows through which women glimpse the sexual possibilities that are open to them. It is nothing more or less than freedom of speech applied to the sexual realm. Feminism is freedom of speech applied to women's sexual rights.

Both pornography and feminism rock the conventional view of sex. They snap the traditional ties between sex and marriage, sex and motherhood. They both threaten family values and flout the status quo. Because of this, when conservatives look at both feminists and women in porn, they see homewreckers, harlots, and sexual deviants.

In other words, pornography and feminism are fellow travelers. And natural allies.

It is time for the feminist movement as a whole to become "improper" and so outrageous as to suggest that sex can be fun and fulfilling. It is time to take sex out of politics and to put it back into the bedroom, where it belongs. Sex is a private choice, and not a political matter open to a majority vote. It is a rebellious process of self-discovery. And feminists should be adamantly defending those women whose sexual choices are under attack. They should be defending women in pornography.

Modern feminism needs a little less dogma and a lot more heresy.

The starting point of this heretical rebellion is to provide a true defense of pornography. Pornography is now the front battleline where the war between sexual correctness and sexual liberation is being waged. The outcome may well define what sexual choices you and I—and our daughters—will be able to make.

I contend: *Pornography benefits women, both personally and politically.*

It benefits them *personally* in several ways:

1. It provides sexual information on at least three levels: it gives a panoramic view of the world's sexual possibilities; it allows women to "safely" experience sexual alternatives; and, it provides a different form of information than can be found in textbooks or discussions.
2. Pornography strips away the emotional confusion that so often surrounds real-world sex.
3. Pornography breaks cultural and political stereotypes, so that each woman can interpret sex for herself.
4. Pornography is the great leveler of shame.
5. Pornography can serve as sexual therapy.

Pornography benefits women *politically* in many ways, including the following:

1. Historically, pornography and feminism have been fellow travelers and natural allies.
2. Pornography is free speech applied to the sexual realm.
3. Viewing pornography may well have a cathartic effect on men who have violent urges toward women.
4. Legitimizing pornography would protect women sex workers, who are stigmatized by our society.

Let's examine the remaining arguments one-by-one:

Personal Benefits
1. Pornography provides sexual information
on at least three levels:
It Gives a Panoramic View of the World's Sexual Possibilities.
Pornography provides women with a real sense of what is sexually available to them: masturbation, voyeurism, exhibitionism,

sex with a stranger, in a group, with the same sex, as an act of revenge . . . It has been called "The Hitchhiker's Guide to the Sexual Galaxy." In times of repression and shame, it is sometimes the only source of sex education for the curious, and of sexual validation for the isolated.

It is how-to literature for those who lack real-world experience, as everyone does in the beginning. Consider just one of the dilemmas of inexperienced women. We all hear about oral sex, but what is it? More specifically, how do you give a man a blow job? What about your teeth? Where do you put your hands? Are the testicles involved? How deep is deepthroating? Are you supposed to swallow? How long should it last? Is it foreplay, or a separate sex act?

Men don't have a monopoly on performance anxiety.

Although how-to sex manuals may give descriptions of oral sex, the most accessible and graphic source of information is pornography. By watching videos, you can vicariously experience the techniques of dozens—even hundreds—of women. You can decide which aspects of oral sex appeal to you and which, if any, you find unsavory.

The same is true of most other forms of sexuality, including masturbation. This form of sexual play seems to come less naturally to women than to men, perhaps because men's sexual organs are more exposed. It is not uncommon for women to reach adulthood without knowing how to give themselves pleasure.

Pornography Allows Women to "Safely" Experience Sexual Alternatives.

One of the most benevolent aspects of pornography is that it provides women with a *safe* environment in which they can satisfy a healthy sexual curiosity. The world is a dangerous place. It is a cold place. Reaching out for real-world experience often involves putting yourself at risk.

The world is especially dangerous for young inexperienced

women who are curious and who want to explore—or push—the boundaries of sex. Real-world sex carries the risk of real-world violence at the hands of a stranger. Or at the fists of a man you thought you knew—until the two of you were behind a closed door, or until he was drunk, or . . .

Rape, domestic violence, sexual battery—the list of dangers is long.

By contrast, pornography can be a source of solitary enlightenment. Pornography presents women with their wildest fantasies—from voyeurism to wearing Bo Peep costumes to mock rape. This cornucopia is served up in the privacy of a woman's own bedroom, on a television set that can be turned off whenever she has had enough. She does not have to defend herself against persistent advances, or "give in" rather than be hurt by a man who will not take no. She is in absolute control of the timing, the content, the duration, the climax.

Pro-pornography women are sometimes accused of not caring about the sexual dangers that face women. I care deeply. I suspect there are few women who have experienced more sexual violence than I have. It is precisely because I know how dangerous the world can be that I have a benevolent view of pornography.

It is because I know how brutal sex can be that I insist on reminding women that they also live in a world of sexual possibilities and pleasures. Sex is too important to surrender. I remember the "sexual revolution" and "women's liberation." Women like me who believed in its promises have been left dazed and wondering where the joy in feminism has gone. The sixties were a period when women were encouraged to enjoy—indeed, to demand!—the bounty of pleasure hidden away within their own bodies.

Many things have happened since then. AIDS and a constellation of other perils have changed sexual mores for us all. But the devastation of AIDS cannot explain the current feminist backlash against the "safe sex" practice of enjoying pornography.

Pornography is *safe* sex. No diseases. No violence. No pregnancy. No infidelity. No one to apologize to the next morning.

Pornography is one of the most benevolent ways a woman can experience who she is sexually.

Pornography Provides a Different Form of Information than Textbooks or Discussion.

Pornography is more than just an encyclopedia of sexual alternatives. It provides women with a different type of information than they can get from a textbook. It offers the emotional information that comes only from experiencing something either directly or vicariously. It provides us with a sense of how it would "feel" to do something.

If pornography offered only intellectual knowledge, it would be far less useful. After all, women already can discuss any sexual theme they wish and still remain "respectable." So long as the sexual expression remains a scholarly discussion, the law takes no notice of what women say. For example, a woman can declare, "I am a lesbian, because it is the purest expression of woman's dignity and true nature." Such a statement is not only acceptable, it is often applauded. But let lesbianism be portrayed in words or images which are meant to be vicariously enjoyed, and the legal system perks up its ears. Knowing about a sexual preference is one thing. Experiencing it is quite another. Even if that experience is vicarious.

Some people believe that open discussion should be enough to provide women with information about sex. But a crucial element is missing. Women still don't have a sense of how it feels—and feeling is what sex is all about. Sex is not about intellect; it is about emotions. Women who watch pornography acquire emotional knowledge about themselves. By indirectly experiencing a wide range of sexual scenarios, they discover their reaction to them.

If a woman listens to a lecture on bondage, she will learn

which activities constitute that subgenre of sexuality. She may come to a conclusion about what she thinks about bondage.

But if she sees a movie in which a woman straps a man down, the images will spark emotional responses. She will move closer to discovering how she feels about bondage. Perhaps the sight of a man tied down to a bed appeals to a woman who has never felt sexual power. Perhaps she is frightened or repelled by the sight. Even these reactions—usually considered negative—are valuable. They indicate where that woman draws the line dividing pleasure from pain, excitement from disgust.

In an essay entitled "Talk Dirty to Me," Sallie Tisdale gave a sense of the emotional information she derives from watching pornography:

"Not all I felt was arousal. There are other reasons for a hurried blush. . . . I felt a heady mix of disgust and excitement, and confusion at that mix. Layers peeled off one after the other, because sometimes I disliked my own response . . . when my body is provoked by what my mind reproves."[2]

2. Pornography strips away the emotional confusion that so often surrounds real-world sex.

It is important to emphasize: Pornography is not real. Pornography is words and images. It allows women to enjoy scenes and situations that would be anathema to them in real life. Women who could never handle the guilt and emotional pressures of an affair can indirectly experience the thrill of one. And feel no shame in doing so.

Why? Because pornography is fantasy. And fantasy is not just some form of attenuated reality. Like dreams or metaphors, sexual fantasies cannot be taken at face value; they should not be taken literally. A woman who daydreams about seducing her neighbor might be genuinely horrified if a glimmer of interest appeared in *his* eyes. A prudish woman might fantasize about a wild threesome in which she throws her inhibitions into a corner along with her clothes; if such a situation cropped up, she might run, with all sincerity, in the other direction.

A fantasy is a wholly artificial situation. It is artificial in a number of ways. For one thing, there are no real-world consequences. By this, I mean: No diseases are communicated; no romantic spur-of-the-moment promises are made; no marriage vows are broken; no children result; no disturbing intimacy is possible. All the dilemmas of real sex are avoided.

The woman exercises a level of control that is never possible in the real world. If the sexual action in a video distresses her, she can hit the off button. If it bores her, she can fast-forward. The characters that draw her are just that: characters. They are not real people to whom she must apologize or send thank-you notes the next morning. They are not people about whom she needs to tell her husband. Pornography is innocent exploration.

Pornography allows a woman's imagination to run wild. And nothing on earth is more human than wondering "what if." It allows women to wonder, What if . . . I were lesbian . . . into leather . . . a virgin again . . . ? What if all the worries and criticism of the world fell away, how would I react to sex then?

Pornography can help us become more self-aware sexually. When we are ready to reach out to another human being, it will not be out of ignorance. It will spring from informed desire.

3. Pornography breaks cultural and political stereotypes, so that each woman can interpret sex for herself.
Women who enjoy pornography are often contemptuously dismissed as "psychologically damaged" by the new feminist puritans. This is especially true if the depiction they enjoy shows something which is considered especially "degrading." The epitome of such a scene is one in which a man ejaculates onto a woman's face.

But judgments like "degrading" do not come from anything objective within the pornography itself; they come from the subjective evaluation of the observer. Degradation, like beauty, is in the eye of the beholder.

For example, when I view pornography in which a woman seems to get real pleasure out of fellatio, it never occurs to me that the woman is psychologically damaged. It never occurs to me that she has fallen in love with her own oppression. I wonder how it feels.

Anti-porn feminists undoubtedly believe that my identification with her pleasure is nothing more than evidence of *my* psychological damage. I contend that the woman who enjoys fellatio represents a totally different interpretation of a blow job than that offered by anti-porn feminism. She represents a different opinion in action.

Pornography can be likened to dreams or other nonliteral forms of expression. Interpretation is extremely personal. Even those sexual acts which are considered to be *prima facia* degrading to women—like ejaculating on a woman's face—are wide open to interpretation. Radical feminism considers such an act to be the quintessential humiliation of women—case closed. It is the subordination of a woman to a man's pleasure, which puts him in a position of power.

But is it?

Consider the perspective offered by James R. Petersen on come-shots: "What makes ejaculating on the outside degrading . . . while ejaculating inside . . . sacred? Do guys learn to come on a woman from porn or from premature ejaculation? . . . For that matter, masturbating guys ejaculate on their own bodies all the time, and not one says, 'Oh God, I just degraded myself.' "[3]

Many interpretations can be attached to coming on a woman's face. In the introduction to *Perspectives on Pornography: Sexuality in Film and Literature,* Gary Day offers a Freudian (and unsatisfying) analysis: "For what the man does in ejaculating over the woman is in a sense to replicate the role of the mother giving milk to the infant. . . . [P]ornography does not show, as some feminists have claimed, a hatred of women but rather a desire to become like them."[4]

Other people—more attuned to the commercial aspects of pornography—claim that come-shots are there purely and simply to prove that the male *did* ejaculate, that he was excited by the sex act. The woman's response of smearing the sperm or tasting it is nothing more than proof that *she* enjoyed and approved of the act.

Still others observe that women are particularly interested in seeing come-shots because men's ejaculations are generally hidden from them. In "normal" sex, women never see men come. To some of them, it may be as seductively elusive as the glimpse of a breast or lace pantie is to a pubescent boy. In this context, the come-shot can be interpreted as almost romantic: The woman wishes to share in her lover's orgasm.

My point is not that any one interpretation is "correct," but that the delightful diversity of human nature allows for many interpretations, none of which are inherently right or wrong. They are all subjective. They are all benign.

But, if any one interpretation should be given extra weight, I think it should be the view of those attuned to the particular subgenre of pornography being viewed. People outside a subgenre cannot realistically judge its nuances any more than people who dislike cheese can judge Brie. After all, when fantasies are not arousing, they all tend to seem ridiculous.

For example, I now understand gay pornography only because gay friends went to the trouble of explaining what particular interactions and pieces of dialogue meant. They knew the slang, the body language, the literary/movie references, the rituals of being gay. Until they clued me in, I felt like a tourist who only barely spoke the language. I suspect the same is true of other subgenres, like S/M; they can be best understood and explained by those who appreciate them.

The appeal of S/M cannot be explained by people like me, who cannot get past a bad reaction to scenes like a man licking a woman's boot. I see nothing of the tease and the flow of mock power that's supposed to be there. I only see what the act would mean to me; and this reaction rather misses the point. The point is: Not everyone responds the way I do.

When I try to open up to it, I can almost understand the attraction of S/M. I know the appeal of scratching the back of a man on top of you, of biting a shoulder, of wrestling on the floor or making up after a fight. A vast number of people find such mild and harmless "violence" stimulating. Why shouldn't a small minority of them enjoy carrying it one step farther?

But when a fantasy expresses violence, people hesitate to acknowledge that it can be benign and beneficial. Take, for example, one of the most common fantasies reported by women—the fantasy of "being taken," of being raped.

The first thing to understand is that a rape fantasy does not represent a desire for the real thing. It is a *fantasy.* The very definition of the word distinguishes it from reality. In a fantasy, the woman is in control of the smallest detail of every act: the timing, the setting, the words, and how she reacts to them. She picks a man to whom she is attracted. If the scene begins to frighten her, she stops it.

In other words, the fantasy has no connection with genuine violence, which strips away control. Rape fantasies offer absolute control to women: They are the opposite of the real thing. To assume that a fantasy of rape reveals a desire to be attacked is like taking a literal interpretation of dreams. Dreaming of a house on fire doesn't make anyone an arsonist.

Why would a healthy woman daydream about being raped? There are dozens of reasons. Perhaps by losing control, she also sheds all sense of responsibility for and guilt over sex. Perhaps it is the exact opposite of the polite, gentle sex she has now. Perhaps it is flattering to imagine a particular man being so overwhelmed by her that he *must* have her. Perhaps she is curious. Perhaps she has some masochistic feelings that are vented through the fantasy. Is it better for her to bottle them up?

The real question to ask is: Why not simply let women enjoy their fantasies? Why shouldn't a woman entertain the wildest sex her imagination can generate? What damage is done? Who has the right to question it?

There is an important corollary. If women's fantasies cannot be taken at face value, neither can men's. Just as a woman's fantasy of rape may represent a desire to surrender without guilt, so too a man's fantasy may show his desire to conquer without consequence. In her book *Magic Mommas, Trembling Sisters, Puritans and Perverts*, Joanna Russ speculates:

"I think male pornography in which a woman is 'raped' . . . may be struggling with a similar problem of permission. . . . Women, after all, fantasize 'rape' as the solution to issue of permission and forced passivity; why shouldn't men . . . use the other side of the same fantasy?"[5]

In fantasy, anything goes—because everything happening in your own mind is inescapably, and *by definition*, "between consenting adults."

4. Pornography is the great leveler of shame.

Historically, women have been made to feel ashamed of their sexual thoughts and desires. Those who were not put on a pedestal were often thrown into the gutter. Women who had the courage to pursue their own sexual pleasure were branded as sluts, whores, and tramps.

As recently as the fifties, respectable women were given the sexual choice of marriage or celibacy. Anything else meant ostracism. Women who demanded pleasure in sex were condemned as "nymphomaniacs," much as they are pitied today as "victims of male culture" by anti-porn feminists.

As a teenager, I struggled with who I was sexually. (This, despite the fact that my sexual preferences fall well within statistical

norms.) I turned to feminism for encouragement and enlightenment. I was lucky. Back then, feminism still offered a vision of
sexual liberation, not of sexual oppression and bitterness. Feminism still had a sense of rollick and raunch, which was invigorat-
ing. I met women who were as confused as I was by sex, men, and
their responses to both. We had late-night sessions over wine
during which we hashed it out.

I worry about the younger generation of women who have to
go through the same sexual angst that confronts us all. If they
turn to feminism, will they find a sense of joy and adventure? Or
will they find only anger and a theory of victimization? Will anti-
porn feminists call their deepest desires "degrading"? Will their
fantasies of rape or being dominated be labeled in political terms
as "the eroticization of oppression"? How much of themselves
will they have to disown in order to be sexually correct?

It is left to pornography to strip away the sexual guilt and confusion that radical feminism heaps upon women who have the
"wrong" sexual responses. Anti-porn feminists tell women to be
ashamed of their appetites and urges. Pornography tells them to
accept and enjoy them. Pornography provides reassurance and
eliminates shame. It says to women, "You are not alone in your
fantasies and deepest darkest desires. Right there, on the screen
are others who feel the same urges and are so confident that they
flaunt them."

If you love to give blow jobs, pornography applauds you. If
you wonder about sex with a woman, pornography makes it
seem harmless. If you wish to be overpowered by a man, porn
allows you to see what it might look like. Videos make no comment on which sexual preferences are acceptable; they eroticize
every aspect of the human body, from feet to breasts; no sexual
question is wrong to ask; no sexual preference is wrong to pursue. Pornography is the true arena of tolerance.

It is also the great leveler of shame. It says, "Sex is good for its
own sake." This is particularly important today, when sex educa-

tion seems to dwell exclusively on sexual negatives: AIDS, disease, teen pregnancy, molestation, date rape, etc. Pornography balances the picture by reminding us that sex can be fun.

Can women afford to do without this essential element of human happiness? I say no.

5. Pornography can serve as sexual therapy.

Pornography enhances the enjoyment of masturbation and provides a sexual outlet for those who—for whatever reason—have no sexual partner. Perhaps they are away from home, recently widowed, or isolated because of infirmity. Perhaps they simply choose to be alone. Sometimes, masturbation and vicarious sex are the only acceptable alternatives to celibacy.

Couples also use pornography to enhance their relationships. Sometimes they do so on their own, watching videos and exploring their reactions together. Sometimes, the couples go to a sex therapist who advises them to use pornography as a way of opening up communication on sex. By sharing pornography, the couples are able to experience variety in their sex lives without having to commit adultery.

The social commentator Fred Berger wrote of the need for variety. He wrote of sex being routine, dull, and unfulfilling. He ascribed this "neurosis" to the constraints on sex imposed by conservatives. "Those constraints dictate with *whom* one has sex, *when* one has sex, how *often* one has sex, *where* one has sex, and so on. Moreover, the web of shame and guilt . . . destroy[s] its enjoyment, and . . . our capacity for joy and pleasure through sex."[6]

Even those of us who never find sex "dull" need variety. In fact, an adventurous spirit may be absolutely necessary to retain the zing in marital sex. Many women are like me. I am not interested in pursuing variety through a series of affairs, which would involve hurting and lying to someone I love. I want to go through decades of sharing new experiences with the same man. I want to tackle head-on the hard problem of keeping sex fresh and playful through a relationship that extends into old age.

Toward this end, pornography is a valuable tool which I do not hesitate to use.

Political Benefits
1. Historically, pornography and feminism have been fellow travelers.

Through much of their history, women's rights and pornography have had common cause. The fates of feminism and pornography have been linked. Both have risen and flourished during the same periods of sexual freedom; both have been attacked by the same political forces, usually conservatives. Laws directed against pornography or obscenity, such as the Comstock laws in the late 1880s, have always been used to hinder women's rights, such as birth control. Although it is not possible to draw a cause-and-effect relationship between the rise of pornography and that of feminism, such a connection seems reasonable to assume. After all, both movements demand the same social condition—namely, sexual freedom.

Chapter Three provided perspective on this.

2. Pornography is free speech applied to the sexual realm.

Freedom of speech is the ally of those who seek change; it is the enemy of those who seek to maintain control. Pornography is nothing more or less than freedom of speech applied to the sexual realm. It is the freedom to challenge the sexual status quo. Pornography, along with all other forms of sexual heresy, such as homosexuality, should have the same legal protection as political heresy.

This protection is especially important to women, whose sexuality has been controlled by censorship through the centuries.

In recent decades, this control has slipped. Abortion is available on demand. Lesbianism no longer means ostracism. Nonmarital sex is commonplace.

But now the barriers to sexual expression are being erected again. The attack is directed not only at pornography, but at other sexual choices as well.

Our society is teetering on the brink of a revolution in sexuality, which is being ushered in by new reproductive technologies (NRTs). Through such techniques as embryo transplants and *in vitro* fertilization, women in their sixties are now able to bear children. Soon there will be new family categories: sperm donor fathers, postmenopausal mothers, test-tube babies. The NRTs will redefine terms like motherhood and the family.

Women are on the verge of being freed from the barriers imposed upon them by nature. Thanks to technology, human sexuality is about to enter the twenty-first century, where a woman's reproductive choices may expand in almost unimaginable ways.

This revolution in sexuality is being opposed by the same feminists who attack pornography. And for the same reason. Both the NRTs and pornography are condemned as "men controlling and exploiting the bodies of women."

As Janice Raymond approvingly states in her book *Women as Wombs*: "Radical feminists stress how male supremacy channels women into pornography and surrogacy as well as into other reproductive procedures. . . ."[7]

On every front, a woman's right to define and to pursue her own sexual destiny is being questioned. Anti-pornography feminists, such as Janice Raymond and Gena Corea, are also in the forefront of an anti-NRT crusade. The attacks on both issues have the same ideological root: the dogmatic belief that there is only one proper way to view sex. Their way.

Pornography threatens this orthodoxy. For doing this, it should be prized all the more.

3. Viewing pornography may well have a cathartic effect on men who have violent urges toward women.

Pornography may be a catharsis for men with violent urges toward women. If this is true, restricting pornography removes a protective barrier between women and abuse.

Studies on rape differ, but many indicate that pornography may prevent violence against women.

Unbiased research on violence against women is desperately needed. Unfortunately, one of the casualties of the new dogma of sexual correctness has been good solid work in this area.

The Kinsey study listed seven different types of rape. However, it is no longer sexually correct to conduct studies on the many causes of rape, because—as any "right thinking" person knows—there is only one cause: patriarchy as expressed through pornography. As the slogan goes, "Pornography is the theory, rape is the practice."

Studies such as the Kinsey report are no longer possible in the sexually correct environment of modern universities. By demonizing pornography, radical feminists are doing women a great disservice. They are blocking valuable research into other possible causes of rape, which could lead to new forms of prevention.

And they are diverting attention away from the real issues underlying violence against women.

In *Magic Mommas, Trembling Sisters, Puritans and Perverts,* Joanna Russ explains: "[P]arallels can be drawn between today's anti-pornography movement and the 19th century Temperance movement. . . . By pinpointing Demon Rum as the central issue, reformers could avoid the real (and dangerous) ones like women's position in marriage and women's lack of economic autonomy. . . ."[8]

The real cause of rape is not pornography, patriarchy, or men as a class. It is the individual men who rape individual women. Pornography is a scapegoat.

4. Legitimizing pornography would protect women sex workers,
who are stigmatized by our society.

Anti-pornography feminists are actually undermining the safety
of sex workers when they treat them as "indoctrinated women."
Leonore Tiefer, a professor of psychology has observed: "These
women have appealed to feminists for support, not rejection.
. . . Sex industry workers, like all women, are striving for economic survival and a decent life, and if feminism means anything
it means sisterhood and solidarity with these women."[9]

The law cannot eliminate pornography, any more than it has
been able to stamp out prostitution. But making pornography illegal *would* further alienate and endanger women sex workers.
Anti-porn feminists realize that laws will simply drive porn
underground. Even totalitarian regimes, with absolute control of
the press and the media, cannot suppress pornography.[10] Indeed,
making it forbidden fruit may increase its attraction.

Anti-porn feminists also know that most of the danger confronting sex workers comes from social stigma, which isolates
them. Without recourse to unions or to the police, performers
have little control over their working conditions. Making pornography illegal—driving the industry underground—will take
away whatever safeguards for women presently exist. Women in
porn would become even more reluctant to go to the police for
protection or to the courts for redress.

Women who were involved in pornography in the fifties,
when it was illegal, tell horror stories of police raids in which
they were made to lie naked and face-down, while police pressed
guns against their heads. The purpose: to make them answer
questions about friends and associates. By trying to drive pornography underground, anti-porn feminists are encouraging a
return to such violence against women sex workers.

In March 1985, a representative of the U.S. Prostitutes Collective stood before the Los Angeles County Board of Supervisors
and pleaded with them *not* to pass an ordinance against pornog-

raphy. She explained that the closure of such sex operations would force the women, who needed to eat and pay their bills, out into the streets as prostitutes. There, they would fall prey to pimps and police crackdowns. She explained: "Feminists who support the porn ordinance said they are not attacking prostitutes—yet the ordinance explicitly calls for enforcement of the prostitution laws. They can't have it both ways."

Pornography needs to be legitimized so that women sex workers can be protected by the legal system, not victimized. Keeping the industry visible is the best way to monitor how women within it are treated. It is the only way to bring public opinion to bear on abuses.

CONCLUSION

After any defense of pornography, a question invariably arises: Is *no* form of pornography objectionable?

On a political and legal level, the answer is: No form of pornography between consenting adults is objectionable. Pornography is words and images, over which the law should have no jurisdiction.

On a personal level, every women has to discover what she considers to be unacceptable. Each woman has to act as her own censor, her own judge of what is appropriate.

"A woman's body, a woman's right" carries certain responsibilities.

SEVEN

INTERVIEWS WITH WOMEN
IN PORN

*"Empirically, all pornography is made under conditions of
inequality based on sex, overwhelmingly by poor, desperate,
homeless, pimped women who were sexually abused as children."*
—Catharine MacKinnon, *Only Words*

With all the voices shouting about pornography—pro and con—
the ones least heeded are those of women who work in the industry. Usually, when you want to know about something, you ask
people who have first-hand experience of it. With pornography,
however, most of the theories come from people who are "outsiders," with no direct knowledge of the industry.

I am open to this charge, as well. To provide a balance for my
own inexperience, I interviewed women in the industry. I didn't
expect to like them as much as I did. As much as I do.

I could claim that I plunged into my research with no precon-
ceptions, but this would be a lie. My assumptions about the
women had been formed by decades of television, movies, and
trashy novels. I expected porn actresses to be hardened, uneducated, abused, and promiscuous women. Although some of them
might have "hearts of gold," they were women who had nothing

to offer but their bodies. I know I expected this by how surprised I was not to find it.

I have less excuse than most people do for being so reactionary. When I was eighteen, my best friend was an older and far more experienced woman named K., who had red hair, green eyes, a stacked body, and a benevolent spirit. Over a Mexican dinner one night, K. explained she was financing her way through grad school at UCLA by working in a massage parlor.

She told this to me because something was worrying her and she needed a friend with whom to talk it over. A few years earlier, she had acted in a porn movie-short by the well-known director, Damiano. Recently re-released, the movie had been reviewed in the latest issue of *Playboy*. The critic had panned it, but he'd singled K. out for praise by name. Unfortunately, she'd used her real one. Now that she was closing in on a Ph.D., K. didn't want to carry the stigma attached to sex work. As a masseuse, she was anonymous; as a porn actress, her name was in *Playboy*.

Talking to K. constituted a crash course on sex for me. It was a friendship from which I am still deriving benefits.

For example, during a recent phone interview with a somewhat reserved porn actress, I mentioned my friendship with K. The conversation stopped abruptly. A cautious question came back from the ear piece. "How did you react to her stories about the massage parlor?" I could tell I was being tested.

"I was jealous," I admitted. "K. was older than me, prettier, and much better with men. I figured she knew something I didn't."

The relief on the other end of the phone line was palpable. I had passed the test. I was a "straight" woman who didn't make moral judgments. Being puzzled, jealous, threatened, and intrigued—all of these reactions were acceptable, because they were honest and not insulting.

The woman warmed to my questions and the quality of the interview improved dramatically.

Upon hanging up, I started to realize how deeply women in porn have been hurt by the condemnation they have received from women outside the industry. Even those few feminists who are supposed to "champion" the rights of sex workers tend to treat them as somehow pathetic. As a class apart. Not as women with husbands and children, unpaid phone bills, and sick pets. Not like all the rest of us.

Few feminists seem willing to grant them the simple courtesy of respecting their choices. Few of them believe women in porn have anything of value to say about sex or politics or human relationships. Certainly, this was true of me before I actually met the women and found so many of them to be articulate.

Part of the schism that separates women in porn from the women on the outside is simply culture shock. Pornography is a dramatically different world and it is easy to misinterpret it. For example, in the corporate world, commenting on a woman's body or calling her "honey" might lead to a lawsuit. In porn, it is standard practice. In fact, an actress might become insecure or insulted if her flaunted assets were ignored. Bernie Oakley of Adam and Eve, the major distributor of adult videos in America, told me that—as a southerner—he had referred to women as "girls" for years. He went to great pains to break this habit only to find himself working in an industry in which the women are *always* called "the girls."

Take another example. While I was speaking to "Jane" at the CES, a well-developed porn actress walked by us. "Jane" stopped talking, ran her tongue over her upper lip, and smiled at me, saying, "Isn't she a walking wet dream?" I was speechless. I wouldn't have known how to respond to a man who'd made such a comment. But a woman? I was at a loss.

Do these differences make pornography a bastion of sexism? Maybe. But compared to what? To corporate boardrooms or government corridors, where men mouth the proper attitudes while maintaining the sexist status quo? Perhaps pornography is just more open about its attitudes.

Moreover, in pornography, women are starting to make a real impact; there are women directors like Veronica Hart and Candida Royalle, whose work was described in *Time* magazine as "the best example of porn in the feminist style." Women like Betty Dodson and Fanny Fatale are empowering women through videos that teach masturbation. And, recently, Femme Distribution, Inc. announced a new series of adult videos by women directors, which—among other things—eroticize safe sex. This is the cutting edge of women's sexuality; feminists ignore it at their own peril.

But entering this world—even as a tourist—can be disorienting and disturbing. The women are not always friendly. I have had my share of curt dismissals, unreturned phone calls, and outright suspicion. It would be a miracle if women who have been stigmatized by feminists reacted less defensively. I learned to begin every conversation with the name of a mutual acquaintance that served as a reference. I made a point of knowing something about the woman, so I could open with a knowledgeable compliment.

"I'll have to check you out" was a common response to my requests for an interview. And even when I supplied referrals and copies of my articles, some women declined to discuss their work with me. Some may have thought I wanted intrusive details about their personal lives, which they wanted to jealously guard. Others may have suspected I would put an unflattering slant on the interview. Even women on the fringe of the industry were often suspicious of me. The business manager of Vivid Video was cautious for no other reason than that I wanted to interview *her* and not the actresses working for the company. For her, this made alarm bells ring.

At first, I thought it odd that the women seemed more suspicious of me than the men did, until I realized the explanation. *I* was a woman. A short, petite, youngish woman who was asking the men for information—in short, for help. I kick-started the "macho" response that typifies much of the porn industry.

Rereading the last line makes me uncomfortable. Next to nothing really "typifies" the porn industry, which is in transition. It is moving from the old school of pornographers to the Young Turks. From cinema verité to home porn. From a male bastion to feminist videos. The entire industry is in flux.

In the same sense, nothing seemed to really typify the women involved in porn. Not one of them was interchangeable with any other. Not one actress had the same story. Some performed sex scenes only with their boyfriends or with other women. One actress had her mother babysit her four-year-old child on the set of her videos. There were four actresses living with a male manager whose real given name was "Lucky." One woman lamented leaving prostitution for the less profitable and more impersonal world of pornography, but—after two arrests for soliciting—what else could she do?

In trying to paint a collective portrait of "women in porn," I run the risk of losing the sense of their rebellious individualism. To prevent this, I wish to present a few of the flesh-and-blood women who breathe life into pornography.

BOBBY LILLY

During my weekend at the Winter Consumer Electronics Show, I heard a common refrain: "You *must* meet Bobby Lilly." The woman wasn't difficult to find. Her flouncy black-and-white polka-dotted dress might have been flashy at most events, but Bobby looked downright conservative as she politicked her way through the aisles of scantily-clad actresses. She and I connected at a meeting of the Free Speech Coalition, just after I had badly mangled my first attempt at an interview. Because she spoke, and eloquently, on the same political issues as I did, I immediately relaxed and regained some of the confidence I had lost moments before.

Hopefully, Bobby Lilly can act as a bridge for readers, as well.

A political activist, Bobby is the moving force behind the Californians Act Against Censorship Together (Cal-Act), which defends "our right to free expression, especially sexual expression." She is also a partner in a three-way marriage between porn superstar Nina Hartley and a man who seems to prefer standing in the background. Bobby is not an actress, but she has appeared in a porn video. She explained why:

"To defend it [graphic sexual expression] without being willing to partake and play a role in it . . . only taking the position 'I'll defend it, but it's not right for me' . . . I just couldn't do it. I had to have the experience. I had to see what it would feel like. And, for me, it was very enjoyable. I found an exhibitionist streak in me that I did not realize was there."

Was she coerced into the industry?

"Oh, absolutely not. It came out of my relationship with Nina. I had been offered a role in an adult video, which had significant redeeming social value because it dealt with people over forty who still had sex lives. And it was done in conjunction with a sex therapist and a book the therapist had written. So I really felt very good about the final product and how it would be used."

Bobby's first experience is probably not typical. She was already familiar with many of the people on the set and had personal values that made her comfortable with nudity and non-monogamous sex. I asked whether anything about the experience disturbed her. "There were things I did not totally appreciate. I mean, every time you go in to a job you can't do everything the way you want to, but that's the right and the role of the director: to decide the order, and that's fine."

Did she know any women who had been coerced into porn? "I do not personally know of anyone, however I know it does exist and I have heard an apocryphal story here and there. But that's not the norm. The level of coercion is very subtle, a very peer-pressure kind of thing."

This is the answer I heard again and again. No one seemed to personally know anyone who had been physically coerced into a pornographic act. But some women spoke of psychological or economic coercion. By "psychological coercion," they usually meant that inexperienced actresses found themselves on a set where they were asked to perform unexpected sex acts. The women could have walked off, but peer pressure is difficult to resist, especially for newcomers who are eager to please.

By "economic coercion" they meant that many women are into porn only to make the money they need to give themselves and their children a decent standard of living. In this, pornography is similar to any other highly paid industry which attracts people who want the money.

I sensed a paradox. Women said there was a lot of money in porn, yet most actresses earned appallingly little for appearing in videos. The standard flat fee for a full day's work is a few hundred dollars; royalties and residuals are unknown. Even superstars rarely make over a thousand dollars a day. Since the cheaper videos are shot in one day and the high quality ones only take a few days more, even hardworking actresses find it difficult to make a fortune.

Bobby explained that the real money to be made from porn was in the dance circuit. What was the dance circuit? "There are many different agencies and clubs around the country, to which adult actresses or *Playboy* centerfolds and what they call 'the big tit girls' travel in a circuit. It's not a circuit in that you go to one place first and then to another. But women book various club dates and go from town to town, dancing. Sometimes they are on the road for weeks or months.

"Many women go into pornography, particularly into videos, to become part of the dance circuit, because porn gives them status and increases their pay for dancing. So the payoff for a video is that, when that box cover gets out into the market and people see it, the actress can get big weekly paychecks on the circuit."

I remembered reading a newspaper article about a woman named Amy Lynn Baxter, a *Penthouse* centerfold who had been lucky enough to be promoted by Howard Stern on a national television program. A high school graduate, Amy had been earning close to $250,000 annually by working about two months a year as an erotic dancer on the dance circuit. With the new publicity, she was hoping to boost that to $500,000 this year, putting her in the same financial bracket as prominent women doctors and lawyers. Whenever Amy travels, she takes both her baby and a nanny.

(And since it is a question that comes up—I should mention that I saw no indication of prostitution being part of the dancers' arrangements.)

I made a mental note to ask dancers I interviewed about "the circuit," then I pushed further on the idea of economic coercion. Specifically, did Bobby know of any producers who refused to pay women who said no?

"On one occasion and it was very unusual.

"One thing people have to understand about this industry is that it has only been legal for about twenty years and it is becoming more . . . 'bureaucratized' isn't the right word . . . 'proper procedures' are now being followed. Ten years ago, when videos started, a lot of people never even thought about paying taxes. Now taxes are being withheld ahead of time. Relationships in the industry are conforming to the regime of society."

What about women who become disillusioned by pornography and want to move on to legitimate film or theater? Bobby acknowledged that "crossovers" happen for technical or support workers, like make-up people. But for actresses? . . .

"Rarely. Porn work does not give you any credentials; in fact, it stigmatizes you. There is no real stigma attached to technical work. I've been on porn sets where the make-up people talk about the legitimate actresses they've made up just days before. But with porn actresses, your biggest example of crossover is Traci Lords, who thoroughly denounces the industry and on that basis has managed to get some roles. A major actor or actress has never become a major Hollywood star."

With this intro into how society stigmatizes porn, I ventured into my main area of disagreement with Bobby: namely, she still believes that the Radical Right ("porn is sin") and not the Radical Left ("porn is violence against women") is the greatest threat to sexual expression today. It is an honest disagreement that comes from our differing experiences. Bobby lives in the San Francisco area where COYOTE has been very effective, largely due to the efforts of sex workers such as Priscilla Alexander and Margo St. James. These women have generated genuine respect within the San Francisco chapter of NOW, which remains sexually liberal.

For better or worse, however, NOW is a decentralized organization in which regions display independence in forging policy and strategy. Liberal chapters like San Francisco and New York have come down with some consistency for the rights of sex workers. But in Texas, for example, the anti-porn membership of NOW did a hostile takeover of the chapter; sexual liberals fled the organization. NOW is clearly in crisis over this issue.

The polarization within feminism has led to the sad spectacle of feminists violently opposing each other on vital issues. For example, the 1992 McConnell Bill—the Victims of Pornography Compensation Act—was supported by radical feminists, yet denounced by the New York chapter of NOW and the Feminists for Free Expression. When a Los Angeles fireman was recently accused of sexual harassment because he read a *Playboy* magazine in his own living quarters while off-duty, NOW supported the sexual harassment charge. Feminists for Free Expression opposed it.

An even sadder spectacle has been that of radical feminists joining with the Religious Right to support legislation, such as the anti-pornography ordinances popular in the eighties. Bobby, who is a child of the Left, lamented, "I'm appalled and frightened by the united front in backing certain legislation, not only against pornography but on the issue of violence in general. What I see happening is that some legitimate concerns within the feminist movement about the abuse of women have been pushed to an extreme by those who say 'we're going to fix it by this process.' Their concern has been taken and used as a battering ram by the right."

I asked Bobby whether she thought the polarization in feminism was getting worse or better?

"I tend to see it leaning toward the pro-sex side, but it may be that I live in California, which is sort of a cutting-edge force, bringing innovative ideas into NOW. For example, this past year, I was able to get a resolution on sexual harassment out of the California State Board that basically took the same position I did. It was a very strong statement about how women are not inherently offended by sexual imagery."

Bobby blamed some of the polarization on how the media has chosen to present the feminist movement.

"The media, for their own reasons, have acknowledged the voices of women such as Catharine MacKinnon and Andrea Dworkin. They have ignored the many women on the other side from Priscilla Alexander to Nan Hunter to porn stars. In my darkest moments, I almost think it is a plot against women. . . ."

I suggested it was a plot for sensationalism—the type of furor that Dworkin stirs up when she proclaims "Every man is a rapist." Bobby threw back, "I think the statement 'All women love sex' should be every bit as sensational."

More thoughtfully, she added: "We have to understand the potential there is [in pornography] for women to speak about ourselves. This has not been tapped. It is only just beginning. If we close the doors to sexual expression, we will never find the connection between sex and our power."

She and I quickly agreed that this power will come as the result of women asserting themselves in porn and insisting on the power of producing and directing. But even without this, Bobby assured me that the industry was responding to the pressure of social criticism:

"For example, about fifteen years ago, it was sort of obligatory to have a rape scene, even if it obviously was a fantasy rape. It is no longer there. There were scenes women found offensive or crude—like being called 'bitch' in the throes of passion. Most of that is gone. There is a sensitivity to complaints and a fear that if there are too many complaints, legal action will be taken under the guise of obscenity. You have to remember that under Reagan and Bush a lot of people in the industry went to jail for sending a videotape across the wrong state line. Now the industry is going to an opposite extreme in self-censorship. Pressure from women, inside and outside the industry, is a part of this."

I asked whether most women in the industry consider themselves to be feminists.

"Most of them don't, no. They believe in equality. But like many mainstream American women, they don't see themselves as bra-burning and man-hating. They have bought into that media stereotype. Yet when you ask them how they feel on issues affecting women, they come down on the side of women's rights."

These are the same women who receive the least protection and respect from society. I mentioned reading an account in the Cal-Act Newsletter about porn actresses whom the police had terrorized. I assumed the incident had come from the "bad-old days" (twenty years ago) when porn was clearly illegal. Bobby quickly corrected me:

"That was less than ten years ago, here in the state of California. It was during a period in which everyone assumed pornography was legal and so they were shooting a lot of it. Then the Los Angeles DA got the creative idea of charging the producers with pimping and pandering, the actors and actresses with prostitution. On that basis, the police raided sets and arrested people."

In the face of such persecution, women in porn desperately need protection not only—or even primarily—from exploitative producers, but from the police and court system. A first step toward such protection is for women to demand to work only on the basis of contracts. As it stands, the only contracts that exist are releases, which protect the producers by guaranteeing that the women are over eighteen years old. Bobby expanded on this:

"Contracts will help a lot, and they are something that may well happen over the next few years. I know there is a consciousness out there that is open to those things. And as it becomes more common, the established people can say 'Well, I won't work without a contract.' There already are those who are 'contract people,' but usually that means they are signed to a long-term contract, which might be considered indentured servitude. Although they do get a lot of money. A union would be the best sort of contract we could get."

NINA HARTLEY

Being new to pornography, I did not know Nina Hartley was a superstar. I first heard of her in a political context. Nina was one of the Erotic Eleven—eleven women who were arrested in January 1993 in Las Vegas on charges of felony lesbianism and pandering.

The charges resulted from their participation in a live sex act that took place at an after-hours fund-raiser held by the "adult video industry." Most of the women arrested wanted to fight the charges, but they were intimidated by the probability of a conviction, which carried a jail term of six to twelve years. Unfortunately, the man who videotaped the fund-raiser had turned his tapes over to the grand jury, so there was no question that the women had engaged in public sex with each other.

In a phone conversation, Nina described the doubts with which she had entered into the performance that had caused so much grief. The benefit act had been set up to raise money for a good cause. Since everyone in the audience was of age and in the porn industry, the performers were urged to spice up the show. Feeling uncomfortable with a "no-limits" situation, Nina opted for the relatively innocuous role of standing onstage and describing into a microphone how to make love to a woman. Other women acted out her descriptions. Unfortunately, an undercover cop was in the audience; the women were arrested.

Nina characterized the treatment of the women in prison as similar to that of "animals on display in a zoo." She added, "The looking-down-their-noses from the female cops was palpable. They were triple gloving before they touched us because we were brought in on prostitution charges. One woman was body-searched in a non-private area, not taken to a private room to be cavity searched. . . . One woman is a recovering junkie and, because of her arrest on prostitution charges, they took blood samples to test for HIV without her consent. She was saying, 'Don't use that arm, use this arm,' but they disregarded her and she had a tremendous swelling on her arm for several days thereafter because they used a damaged vein. . . . I didn't appreciate that they allowed our real names to be posted, which, for women in our line of work, can be very dangerous."

Eventually, the prosecutor agreed to drop the charges down to a misdemeanor *if* the women pleaded "guilty" and *if* they made a "voluntary" donation of $20,000 to local charities. People in the industry banded together and raised the "donation." But the women still face tens of thousands of dollars in unpaid legal bills.

The repercussions echo on. For example, Nina was recently refused entry into Canada—where she often works as a dancer—because of the misdemeanor conviction. On lawyer's advice, Nina crossed the border as an ordinary citizen and met with fans, without receiving pay. Despite these precautions, Canadian immigration held her in jail for three days and then, after a hearing, a judge gave her thirty days to leave the country.

Fortunately, Nina Hartley's career can weather such storms. Best known as an actress and feature dancer, Nina has recently made the leap into directing.

I caught up with Nina in Atlanta, where she was on the dance circuit. Nina spends two weeks of every month on the road, which she describes as being "too much." Nina began as an erotic dancer over a decade ago while she was going to school to become a nurse. A strong exhibitionist urge led her (and her husband, then boyfriend) to check out a local club, where she was quickly offered a job. Nina had discovered her true vocation.

Nina became involved in the video industry because of what she calls "a long-standing fantasy of creating explicit adult material." This, in turn, sprang from the radical literature she read in her youth, such as *The Joy of Sex* and the feminist classic *Our Bodies, Ourselves.* Nina speaks of sixties feminism as the intellectual "cradle" from which she emerged. Feminism convinced her: "If it's consensual, it's okay," and "Sex is essentially good."

Recently, she directed the video *Nina Hartley's Book of Love.* She also produced the first two in a series of educational/entertainment films. From Adam and Eve, they are titled, *Nina Hartley's Guide to Better Cunnilingus and Fellatio.* Her goal is to infuse pornography with a fresh approach that provides it with a larger context of music and movement, body humor, and theatrical flair. Perhaps even a two-character sexually graphic play.

These ambitions will be difficult to fulfill, since "home porn" and inexpensive videos seem to be dominating the industry at the expense of high-budget movies, such as the classic *Behind the Green Door* with its crafted script and exquisite sets. Videotape has democratized porn and caused a drop-off in artistry, simply because producers no longer have to be filmmakers to rake in the profits. The chains of adult theaters that formerly existed to promote large-budget films—e.g., the Pussycat chain—are almost a memory. Moreover, films like *I Am Curious Yellow* were made two or three decades ago, when women were allowed to be adventurous and kinky. The whole world has become a little bit meaner and less tolerant than it was a few decades ago.

I asked Nina the obligatory question: Have you ever been coerced into a pornographic act?

"No, never, no, goodness." She added, "Like bosses everywhere, some will push at you until you say no. There have been situations where people are emotionally vulnerable and taken advantage of, yes." This is particularly true of the "women who knock on our doors every day, asking if they can be in videos.

"I feel bad for the women who get into pornography not for the fun, but because they seek only economic gain," she continued, "because they are the ones who will be hurt by the experience. They will feel exploited, used, and abused even though they are responsible for putting themselves out there. To do a highly stigmatized activity with a permanent record just for the money . . . this is what causes the real damage."

Women in porn *have* to love what they doing because it is a tough way to make a living. In fact, it is not possible for women to earn a truly decent living just by appearing in videos, because they have to work too many days. Moreover, they usually have to work either in Los Angeles or New York, where living is expensive.

So they get exposure through videos and then take their show on the road, where a feature act can make as much as $6,000 to $10,000 a week. But if they don't get pleasure out of their dancing —if it is just a matter of money—Nina thinks they are selling themselves short. She routinely counsels women who are unhappy with the industry to take a month or two off in order to think about where they are in life and whether they want to continue in pornography.

She calls this her "mother-hen rap." I asked her how she would counsel someone like Linda Lovelace, whom many in the industry seem to dismiss as a liar. "I wouldn't dismiss her. That's how she experienced things. But I would tell her to take responsibility for the situation in which she found herself."

I wondered aloud about violence in pornography. I told her I had been searching through movies, TV channels, and magazines without being able to find anything really offensive. It is difficult to find nasty pornography. Yet I keep reading radical feminists who claim that seventy-five percent, or some comparably huge chunk, of pornography *is* violence, containing scenes of rape or torture. "They are out to lunch on that," Nina replied, "especially on rape scenes; they were passé by '80, '81.

"Ever since the early nineties, when all the obscenity prosecutions were going on, the industry has been paranoid about censoring itself. People have stopped doing anything that might be objectionable. For example, some producers ask actresses not to say 'Oh God, Oh God' when they come in sex scenes.

"Nor do they dare to show a scene that remotely resembles nonconsensual sex. So you have bondage movies which look ridiculous," Nina explained. "Bondage is a pre-orgasmic experience, but most producers will no longer couple it with sex for fear of the hysteria over 'sex leading to violence.' Producers think they have to divide fetish activity from sexual activity. So you have bondage portrayed as something apart from foreplay and sex, which makes the people involved in it seem even more perverted than they did before."

Everything in porn seemed to be skewed to conform with outside pressures. I asked Nina how she, as a porn actress, was treated by mainstream feminists. "As long as the women have an okay attitude about sex to begin with, I am usually treated respectfully. Once they meet me, they realize I am not an idiot, not a sexual-abuse survivor. I'm just a person who can talk about weather, and cars, and kids, and politics. They realize there is an-other side to this business and that not every woman is oppressed who's in it."

In fact, a lot of Nina's fans are women, whom she tells to take responsibility for their own orgasms. "This is the most powerful thing any woman can do. Take responsibility for the timing of lovemaking, the mood that's set . . ." Here she sighs deeply. "But taking responsibility requires a generous heart, and women, right now, are very, very angry. Many do not seem to have the gener-osity in their hearts that is necessary to . . . for want of better words . . . to honor Aphrodite. They are killing their own well of life."

This remark, of course, drifts directly into a discussion of the anti-porn/anti-sex tendencies of modern feminism. Nina sees this as a response to men. Anti-porn feminists actively hate men and blame them for what they see as the "victimization of women." According to Nina, "Pornography, as they under-stand the word, is the ultimate personification of everything that is bad. Actually, their response to porn is a throwback to Judeo-Christian ethics. A true feminist is a compassionate person, who tries to encourage women to speak their own 'truths.'"

But feminists are so angry at men they will not listen to dis-senting opinions—and especially not to men's pain, their voices or their needs. As she put it, "We're still just so angry at them and their penises and their need to put it in us. It is a very anti-sexual response." Their anger prevents feminists from realizing that men are as oppressed as women are by sexual, social, and political attitudes, if only in different areas of sexuality.

I asked Nina if she had ever had a dialogue with an anti-porn feminist, like Dworkin. Nina declines to debate such women, be-cause they are irrational zealots who are not interested in listen-ing to her. "Why should I put myself through that?" Nina's afraid she'd get more flustered than she likes to be in public; instead of arguing, she might just sit there, saying over and over, "You're full of shit, you're full of shit."

About the hatred and fear directed at her by Christians, she seems more philosophical. "These are the people who are truly obsessed with sex. Sex with them is still a very big issue and they are not at all comfortable with it. Then, there I am . . . poking them with a sharp stick." She tries to be sensitive to their pain, but admits that "their pain amazes me, because I have no background on which to pin it." Mostly, she fights an urge to scratch her head and walk away.

Next, I asked about the prospect of women like her rising to positions of power in the industry. "The business is not that old, and back in the seventies men ran everything. The pornography business, like most businesses in the United States, is predominantly male-controlled. However, there has been matriculation up through the ranks and, certainly, Candida Royalle is the most thrilling example of that. Individual women have made individual deals to direct."

But even an actress of Nina's stature does not receive royalties, residuals, or any of the niceties that women in any other branch of entertainment have come to expect from a contract. Indeed, most of her contracts are verbal, not written, because—after all —what court would uphold them? Nevertheless, things are a lot better in porn than they used to be, from small things like providing a hot lunch and a shower after scenes, to large and exciting things like women beginning to direct. "In another twenty years, we might be unionized . . . who knows?"

I pointed out that many reactionary industries have been revolutionized in the last twenty years and women in them are now well represented. But pornography has not kept pace by integrating women into positions of power. She explained, "A lot of the original people are still alive who were in power when it was still illegal." The old guard is the wrong age, the wrong gender, and the wrong attitude to be of assistance to women. Also, porn has been isolated from political and social change because society has pushed it off to one side. One reason for this is that producers of porn do not have advertisers and backers who threaten to withdraw their money, as regular TV or film producers do. "Fortunately," she added, "the pie is huge."

I concluded by asking Nina what was the one thing she wanted women to know about porn. She didn't miss a beat in answering, "Sex isn't something men do to you. It isn't something men get out of you. Sex is something you dive into with gusto and like it every bit as much as he does."

CRYSTAL WILDER

Crystal Wilder was the only woman I interviewed who made me feel protective.

Bernie Oakley of Adam and Eve had given me Crystal's fax number and encouraged me to use his name as an intro—a common method of networking in the industry. He had also provided me with a bit of data on Crystal. She had started out as a dancer and proceeded on to videos as a way to boost herself into "feature dancer" status. I was intrigued to hear she was now in transition from actress to producer, playing both roles in a company she co-owned and operated with her husband. This was a smart woman, who wanted to keep the profits that resulted from her own performances.

Crystal's company, Wilder Productions, is a new business venture that produces X- and R-rated movies. The company's first release is entitled *Wilder at Heart*; the latest one is an R-rated documentary on the Miss Nude Universe Contest. In order to control quality, Crystal's husband handles postproduction, but I was heartened to hear that Wilder Productions uses outside script writers. This means the company is less likely to fall into the trap of producing amateurish films that are shot spontaneously.

In our first phone call, I scheduled a convenient time for Crystal to be interviewed. She was bubbly at the prospect—an enthusiasm that was entirely missing when the appointed time rolled around. From the tone of her voice, I suspected a problem and immediately switched tactics by asking if there was anything she wanted to know about me or the book. Yes, there definitely were things she wanted to know. What was my educational background? What were my qualifications for writing this book?

I realized that in the intervening week Crystal had been having second thoughts, perhaps about my motives or whether she would be fairly treated in the book. Given how most feminists treat sex workers, who could blame her? Fortunately, in porn, the names of those you know often serve as credentials for who you are, and I had carefully constructed a network of solid contacts. I briefly answered Crystal's questions about my credentials, then referred to some prominent people in the industry who had offered me the use of their names as calling cards. Crystal relaxed.

I began by asking if she had ever been coerced into a pornographic act. "Never," the adamant response came back, then her tone softened. "I wondered about that before I was in the business, before I was a dancer, and I'm glad to say 'never.'" Nor did she know of anyone who had been coerced. But she had seen borderline things. While watching a hair-pulling scene, for example, she became convinced that the woman—although technically consenting—was not enjoying herself. She suspected that the woman was new to the business and just going along with whatever the director wanted. "This happens a lot to newcomers," she assured me.

Moving from consent to contracts, I asked what paperwork she was used to signing before making a video. Although the twenty-six-year-old actress had acted in over a hundred videos, she had never signed anything beyond a release, which protected only the director. Crystal worked on the basis of a verbal understanding. So far, no director had refused to pay her, and only a few checks had bounced. Her worst experience? Being shorted money by a club owner in Canada, with whom she *did* have a contract. Knowing that no judge would take her seriously, Crystal wrote the money off. She refers to industry contracts as "a joke," because they are unenforceable.

If she had been shorted by someone in video, Crystal would have had some recourse. A few well-placed phone calls would have resulted in pressure being brought to bear on the erring party. *Adult Video News*—the most influential periodical in the industry—makes a point of gently policing business practices. Powerful men like Phil Harvey, owner of Adam and Eve, are known to take strong ethical stands. But such self-regulation is not the norm on the dance circuit, which crosses borders and is not represented by centralized organizations. There is not the same sense of community.

Having cleared away the obligatory questions about coercion and contracts, I asked Crystal how she got involved in the industry. Her first experience, on the fringe of porn, came when she posed for some magazines. What impressed her the most were the women; they were "very, very nice people." From here, she almost stumbled into exotic dancing: She and her husband were on vacation and happened to go to a dance club in Nebraska. On a lark, Crystal entered a wet T-shirt contest and won $100—a fortune to her at the time. Thus encouraged, she checked out a local dance club, which she found to be clean and tasteful. "Nothing nasty was happening there, and the girls were having a good time."

As for progressing into porn videos—a lot of dancers do this in order to work their way up the financial ladder to "feature dancer." In this, Crystal has been overwhelmingly successful. These days, she travels from club to club with a truckload of over $30,000 worth of lights, which add glitz to such dance routines as the one in which she dresses up like an ice cream sundae and slings her toppings around the stage. As she explains, "I don't want to just take off my clothes. People can see that in a video."

I pulled the conversation back to how Crystal had gone from her first dance club to her first video. "I met an agent," and through him she arranged to make a "couple of movies" to see if she liked the work. At this point, Crystal made a statement to which I would later return and which would ultimately define the interview for me. She said, "I figured if I made only a few of them, no one would know. I didn't want it to be known all over my hometown, I guess." This was a theme I did not immediately pick up on.

Sensing that Crystal's ambitions extended beyond acting in porn—and, perhaps, beyond producing it—I asked whether she wanted to cross over from porn to more legitimate films, like Traci Lords was attempting to do. "Yes," but she felt "branded" from having done porn. This comment, coming on the heels of not wanting it to be known in her hometown, began to flash a red light in my mind.

When I asked what—besides money—made porn worth being branded over, she talked about the dance clubs, where male fans lavished attention on her. "They think I am an ultimate fantasy. Some of them call me a superstar and come into the clubs for no other reason than to see me. It is the greatest feeling in the world," she bubbled on, "to be taken so seriously for something that most people don't see as legitimate. It makes everything worthwhile."

Here it was for the third time. She did not want to be known in her hometown; she felt branded by porn; she was delighted to be *finally* taken seriously. This was a woman who craved acceptance and expected rejection. Yet, Crystal was also clearly proud of her work and craved recognition for it. There was a tension and ambivalence about Crystal that contrasted with the self-confidence of Nina Hartley and the political sophistication of Bobby Lilly. A major male producer had assured me that Crystal lived up to her name: She was "Wilder" than most. To me, she seemed vulnerable.

I picked up on the theme of being branded by porn. I asked how the people in her small midwestern hometown reacted to her being in the industry. "They know about it, but they don't acknowledge it. It is not really discussed, but they accept me because we are family and friends and we were prior to the porn. They realize I'm the same person."

Do they think there is something wrong with you? "Yes." How did you feel about that? "You know what? At first, it really did hurt my feelings, but being brought up in the Midwest, I understand that a lot of people are very closed-minded and it is something that is hard to overcome. As far as what I do, I know my parents look upon it as something totally unacceptable. I can understand them now because I have become a lot more understanding and nonjudgmental . . . but I wish they could open their hearts and understand that I'm doing what I want to do and I'm not hurting anyone."

I wondered aloud whether she had found more acceptance from people since moving from the Midwest to California.

Yes and no. She bonds with other women in the industry, but hardly ever tells outside people what she does for a living. She is painfully aware that "regular" women view her as an "outcast." This keeps her from getting active in political or social causes, because people might ask her, "And what do you do?"

At one point, I started describing a party I'd attended at which pornography had become a hot topic of discussion. I had a point in mind, but I never managed to reach it, because Crystal broke in. "I really miss going to things like that," she said.

"It [the ostracism] hurts me a lot because I enjoy being around people and having close friends and they [regular women] just can't look at you in the same way once they know what you do. I guess I am just really afraid to get close to women who are not in the industry because I don't like being judged and every time, when I am asked by a female what I do and I'm honest about it, *that look on their face!*... All they are seeing is what I do. They are not looking at me. It's a hard thing to overcome."

As we spoke, Crystal's voice kept sinking until I had trouble hearing her. For the first time in the course of my interviews, I felt impelled to stop being impartial. I just talked to her, like I would to any other human being. I explained that one of the things women in her position do not appreciate is how intimidating and threatening they are to ordinary women—to housewives or even to a happily married career woman like me, who is approaching forty and starting to sag faster than I can prop it up.

I reminded her of what she had said: The men come into the club and say, "You're my ultimate fantasy." Well, most of those men have wives or girlfriends, yet they are saying these words to *her*, not to them. Crystal should understand how that makes these women feel and how easy it is to blame her for it. They are threatened and intimidated.

"The women don't find me intimidating," she objected; "they call me sleazy."

"But if they said, 'You're intimidating,' " I replied, "that would give all the power to you; you're so powerful, you threaten them. If they say, 'You're a sleazy, sick bitch,' that makes *you* the wrong one; it makes you pathetic and not them. When you make people feel insecure, you also make them angry."

Women like Crystal are a socially safe and convenient dumping ground for the jealousy and insecurity of others. Most women cannot live out their fantasies or have what they want sexually. This is the nature of reality: Not many of us can have it all. Perhaps we are not attractive enough or too inhibited or just unlucky. Even women who are reconciled to not having "it all" are likely to resent women like Crystal, in much the same way the poor envy the rich. After all, there she is dressed up like an ice cream sundae, to the applause of their husbands.

The fact that she is happily married doesn't decrease the jealousy. But it does explain something that was puzzling me: How did she escape the somewhat hard polish that I saw in most of the other women. Crystal's husband seems to form a barrier between her and the harshness of the "non-porn" world.

Crystal recounted an incident that occurred at the Canadian border when she and her husband drove up to conduct a three-to-four-week tour. Since she travels with a caravan of lights and equipment, customs routinely checks things out before waving them through. This time they were carrying a few videotapes of Crystal, not for sale—which was prohibited—but to show as promotion. Her husband took responsibility for them and was arrested for attempting to smuggle pornography. (That particular province prohibited anal sex and facial come-shots, both of which were in the videos.) It is little wonder that, when I asked Crystal what she would change about the industry, she immediately replied, "I want a written guide for what is and is not illegal to produce and distribute from place to place."

Crystal's marriage intrigued me. Many porn actresses are married, but she was the first one with what seemed to be a conventional marriage—a monogamous partnership, which included a small mom-and-pop business and the desire for children: the American dream. I was curious, but I had resolved never to intrude into the personal lives of the women I interviewed.

Instead of asking direct questions like, how does your husband feel when he watches you have sex on-screen?, I asked, how do porn actresses such as yourself reconcile on-screen sex with a monogamous marriage? "Many of them restrict themselves to girl–girl scenes or have sex only with their husbands to keep from 'complicating' their marriages."

I wondered aloud whether married men in porn handle things with as much delicacy. Apparently, they didn't, because they don't attach the same importance to sex as women do. "The men in porno are not like your average man, because sex is a job, sometimes mechanical. They are the ones who have to perform as far as the come-shot."

As the interview dissolved into a conversation, I drew it to a close by asking what she wanted to tell other women about pornography. "Just that I don't like getting feedback that's so negative ... But I try not to be judgmental back. I keep asking myself, Who am I to judge?, because I don't like it when people judge me."

CANDIDA ROYALLE

Without question, Candida Royalle is the most powerful woman in pornography today. In 1984, having acted in several porn classics, she founded Femme Productions in order to create sensual adult movies that would appeal to women, allowing them to explore their sexual potential. For example, the promo literature for Femme's futuristic movie *Revelations* reads:

> "Ariel's world is sterile and gray. Creative expression is looked upon with suspicion and sex is only for procreation. Ariel follows the rules as best she can ... until she makes a discovery that will forever change her life. . . . There, kept alive forever on videotapes secretly made by loving couples, are the lives of those who lived in a different time. . . . A time when passions ran freely and people were allowed to express themselves, creatively, sexually, lovingly. . . . What does she do with her sexual awakening in a world where it is forbidden enough to warrant state arrest and imprisonment?"

Women desperately need their own form of pornography. According to a 1989 study by *Adult Video News*—the closest thing the industry has to a Bible—twenty-nine percent of adult video customers were couples and fifteen percent were women; that segment of customers was growing rapidly. Candida addresses this huge audience through award-winning movies, such as *Three Daughters,* which tell a story—complete with original sound-track, soft focus, and few genital close-ups.

Her films are reminiscent of porn classics from the seventies, which were carefully scripted with intricate plots and good acting. There are two reasons for this: Ms. Royalle is willing to spend months, if necessary, developing a concept—*Revelations* took two years—and, her budgets are often ten times larger than those of most adult films. Although the "old guard" of porn claims it is not possible, Candida makes a profit without lowering her staggering sticker price of $79.95 (mail order $39.95). And this, despite the fact that the theater system that formerly supported "big-budget" porn is now dead.

When I asked how she was able to survive, she responded, "... The fact that we are so unique means that our work doesn't live for just one week and then die off and become what they call 'catalog.' The phenomenal thing about our line is that the first movie we ever made in '84 sells as strong as the last movie."

She never lowers her price. Instead, she does an incredible number of interviews and personal appearances to promote Femme Productions.

I caught up with Candida in her office, in a dead period before she dashed out to rehearse for her second career as back-up singer in her boyfriend's rock band. I began by asking why Femme advertised its products as "erotica" rather than pornography. "I like to think that my work takes more of a holistic approach to sexuality and lovemaking. I like to pull away from the obvious hard-core and get to the more subtle nuances of lovemaking. And I like to avoid the word *romance,* because I want to get away from the conception that women *need* romance as part of having sex."

Candida's commitment to women's sexuality led her to create Femme's Star Director Series—a collection of thirty-to-forty-minute short stories which are directed by women superstars such as Gloria Leonard, Veronica Hart, Veronica Vera, and Annie Sprinkle. These women came together in July 1983, when they began a support group for adult film actresses; they went on to become business associates.

Femme's movies blend compelling content with filmmaking niceties such as original sound scores. Gloria Leonard's *Fortune Smiles*, for example, is advertised as taking "us on a touchingly funny walk through the minds of two people who have been dating and are about to take the leap into bed." Candida explains why she took a chance on such an innovative series. "I wanted to give each of these women an opportunity to express their personal views and fantasies about sex, love, and men."

Candida's philosophy is also expressed in the working conditions on her sets. "I bring a respect and compassion to the people who work for me, perhaps because I've been in front of the camera myself." She can remember walking on less pleasant sets as an actress, only to find them filled with sleazy producers/directors she didn't respect. That made her feel sleazy to be there. Candida offers her people respect; in turn, she demands professionalism. She will not hire anyone who has an active history of drugs, alcoholism, or other self-destructive behavior.

Part of this professionalism is a commitment to safe sex, which includes using condoms on the set whenever the couples are not real-life lovers. Candida is the only major producer of heterosexual porn I have found who implements this policy. Femme has used condoms since 1986, when they became standard equipment for two basic reasons: to protect the talent (actors and actresses) and to set the example of a responsible approach.

Candida told me about the only time she breached this safe sex policy. "I remember with Jeanna Fine when we did *Taste of Ambrosia*—she and Randy [Paul] had worked together a lot and I really wanted her to use a condom. She tried, but she really didn't want to use it so I just said, 'Fine, we won't use it.' But I thought,

'This poor woman, she doesn't realize that she should be happy that I'm asking her to do this.' "

Candida went on to explain that if she is filming a dream or fantasy sequence, condoms are still used but the scene is handled differently, because—after all—condoms rarely exist in dreams and fantasies. Camera angles and other techniques mask their presence. In *Rites of Passion,* the sequence directed by Veronica Vera [Shady Madonna] used a condom but the camera didn't go in so tight that you could see it.

Especially when it is clear that couples are getting together for the first time—as in Leonard's story about first-time sex between dating couples—Femme likes to show condoms as being fun, as sex toys. Candida explained how, in the segment of *A Taste of Ambrosia* directed by Veronica Hart, condoms were eroticized. "There was the scene where the woman puts a black condom on the guy and fellates him over it. I always say to people, 'If you think it can't be erotic, look at that scene.' "

It is a sign of how "in control" Candida is that I did not ask my obligatory question about coercion until twenty minutes into the interview. I finally blurted out: "Have you ever been coerced into a pornographic act?"

"No. The only time it ever came close—and it wasn't bad— was when I was working with one of the bigger filmmakers. It was one of the first films I ever did and it was about this big albino guy who, in the story, had been abusing prostitutes. Some women throw an all-night party for him and they get him really drunk. At a certain point, the women all stand over him and pee on him.

"This wasn't in the script and all of a sudden they started handing out beers to all the actresses. Now, I don't drink beer. I don't like the taste of it. So I said, 'Excuse me, what is this?' And I was told that there was a scene in which we were all going to pee on him. I said, 'Excuse me, I did not say I would do that. I was never told I would do it. I am *not* doing it.' " Candida rallied the other women; finally, some of them did the scene and some didn't, depending on whether it offended them. The only coercion used against Candida was the threat that she would never work for him again. She was paid for the work she'd done.

I ask if she knew of any women who had been coerced.

"No."

Then, before I could broach the subject of my next question, she brought it up herself. "Have you read Linda Lovelace's book *Ordeal*?" Candida asked.

"What is shocking to me," she continued upon discovering I had, "is that this is not a book about pornography; it is about domestic violence. It is about a woman who is abused as a child, who marries an abusive man and is turned into a prostitute by *him.* Not by pornography. If you read the book—*in her very own words!*—you find out that the whole thing about a gun to her head came from her own husband and was never part of the set of *Deep Throat.* In fact, she says that making the movie was the first time she felt she could smile, because the people were so nice to her. The reason she ended up with bruises was because her husband was so jealous of how nice they were to her on the set that he beat her up in their hotel room. If any violence had occurred on the set, the crew would have stopped it, but they were so intimidated by him that they didn't say anything about what he did to her after hours.

"Rather than being an indictment of pornography, getting involved in the industry and becoming a star is what enabled her to finally escape. Women Against Pornography grabbed onto her story and acted every bit as exploitative as her husband did. They took her story, and instead of really trying to help the woman, who desperately needed help, they decided to misconstrue the facts and to wave her like a banner for their cause."

As long as the anti-porn cause had come up, I wanted to know whether or not—as a producer—Candida had started to shy away from the sort of scenes that have been criticized as degrading to women, such as come-shots on the face or mock rapes.

This was the only time Candida—a veteran interviewee— paused before giving an answer. On one hand, she doesn't have come-shots on the face in her movies, because it has become standard (thus boring) and because she thinks most women *do* find it degrading. On the other hand, she believes women can get "as down and dirty as the best of them." Besides which, occasionally "playing nasty" with your lover can be good, clean fun. If an actress wanted to do a come-shot on her face, Candida was not sure how she would react.

As for mock rape scenes—she is comfortable enough with them to include them in her films, and believes society misunderstands the distinction between consensual powerplay and real abuse. In fact, her semidocumentary, *LOVERS: An Intimate Portrait*, has a scene of mock rape.

Candida is well aware that anti-porn feminism is a radical departure from the early days of the movement. "I was a very active young feminist in college between '69 and '71. We [The Bronx Coalition] had a storefront, we ran groups, we gave free pap smears once a year, we were really working hard. I finally left the movement because everything was getting full of anger pointed at men. Men did *this* to us, men did *that* to us. At the time, I noticed also that if you had anything to do with men you were basically 'sleeping with the enemy.'

"You know, the feminist movement was so essential to my growth, but I didn't do it to hate men. I did it to better my life. So I left the movement ['72], right around when it was becoming fashionable to be a lesbian. I really see that this [the anti-porn hysteria] is the outgrowth of that. The movement was co-opted by women who decided there was no hope for men, that we really had to be split off from them and that sex was our enemy as well . . . unless it was masturbatory or lesbian."

Candida sighed, "Now we see that 'feminism' has a bad connotation to it for the younger generation: It is anti-man, anti-sex."

The responsibility for this lies with radical feminists like Andrea Dworkin and Catharine MacKinnon. Candida told me about the only time she encountered MacKinnon. It was in 1986, when they were on a panel together on the Donahue show. At that point, Candida didn't know enough about the anti-porn zealot to get the full impact of who she was sitting beside. The show was somewhat stacked against MacKinnon. MacKinnon managed to dig her own grave by talking in impenetrable legalese. Now that Candida knows who these women are, she would love to confront them. But, as she says, "Now none of them will even get on the same stage with someone like me, which is very telling. Norma Ramos loves to call me a 'pimp' on the news."

I asked her what she wanted people to know about the industry. Candida said that society's reaction was a catch-22. People complain about the low quality of porn and pity the "poor" women who work under such awful conditions, but both of these things are caused by society's repression and intolerance. Until this changes—until society grants sex and pornography the legitimacy it deserves—the industry will never attract a high level of filmmaker, who has a social consciousness. As long as pornography is stigmatized, everyone who works in it will be victimized.

BRENDA LOEW TATELBAUM

Historically, the most important vehicle for pornography has been the printed word. Today, as videos and computers assume a leading role in mass distribution, newsprint has become the main haven for less popular forms of sexual expression about which producers are beginning to feel uncomfortable. This seems especially true of sadomasochism (S/M)—the game-playing foreplay that focuses on dominance and mock violence. S/M, with its leather costumes, whips, and snarls has become less welcome in a video industry trying to reassure society that there is no connection between sex and violence.

Newsprint is also the main way people with unusual sexual

preferences contact each other through personal advertisements. Although home porn—the unpolished amateur videos made and marketed by real people—also addresses this need, it does so through the printed word in the form of newsletters, which establish a sense of community.

The published word, like the broadcasted image, faces unique challenges. No one knows this better than publisher/editor Brenda Tatelbaum of Boston, who publishes the sexually graphic *EIDOS* (Everyone Is Doing Outrageous Sex). Brenda may soon be conducting a one-woman crusade against British customs.

Her troubles began in September 1993, when a female subscriber sent *EIDOS* a notice she had received from British customs; the notice declared the magazine to be obscene and duly confiscated under a law dating back to 1876. Ironically, *EIDOS* would be entirely legal if published domestically in England. Brenda wrote a letter of appeal to the British government—the only official course open to her—then contacted such organizations as Feminists Against Censorship and the Libertarian Alliance, to no avail. Indeed, the feedback she's received from some feminists has been hostile.

One feminist organization attacked her for running personal classified ads. Although the spokeswoman had never read *EIDOS*, she accused Brenda of putting women in jeopardy, because criminally intentioned people might answer the sexually oriented ads placed by women. Brenda assured her that in ten years of publishing, such a situation had never arisen. But the woman remained adamantly hostile. Rather than being angry in return, Brenda was baffled. She kept repeating to me, "I just don't get it. They say I'm promoting violence against women. They say images are criminal. I just don't get it."

Brenda is paying the price for promoting an alternate view of sexuality. This is an increasingly unpopular thing to do. As she explained, "With the increasingly centralized distribution of information worldwide—everyone is getting the same messages and images, whether from the newsstand or TV. There is a wall going up against secondary or alternative sources. The alternative press is being driven more and more underground." Soon, there may be only one societally sanctioned view of human sexuality.

In mid-July '94, Brenda's distributor faxed her a letter declaring his intention to refuse further shipments of *EIDOS*. Perhaps because the magazine is popular among Brits with alternate lifestyles, it has been tagged for special treatment. The distributor feared that if shipments of *EIDOS* slipped through customs, officials might raid his home and confiscate not only that periodical, but his entire inventory.

When Brenda called the British Consulate, she discovered she would be liable to arrest if she flew to England and tried to transport *EIDOS* on her person. From former run-ins with U.S. mail authorities, she knows they often "misinterpret" the law to fit their own needs. Accordingly, she is planning to touch down on British soil with the offending material and hold what she hopes will be a reasonable conversation with the officials there. Four alternative publishers in England have promised to run ads publicizing her plight. They are trying to rouse support for Brenda's plans to confront British customs and picket the place, if necessary.

When *Penthouse* faced the same sort of repression from British customs in the seventies, it had the resources to fight in court and win. Brenda has to rely on moral suasion.

With this conflict in my mind, I opened my first issue of *EIDOS:* Volume 7, Number 3—the tenth anniversary issue. Its cover sported the photo of a dominant woman dressed in what appeared to be a lace and leather corset. A muzzled man crouched between her spread legs, one arm wrapped around her ankle. In one hand the woman held a paddle; the other hand had a firm grip in the tangles of the man's hair.

The inner pages contained letters from *The Progressive* and North Carolina State University, as well as the request for a sample copy from the Institute of Scientific Information of the U.S.S.R. Academy of Sciences; news clippings with information on sexually oriented news items, such as the ongoing abortion struggle; and notices of seizure by British customs. There was an extensive poetry section with titles like "Pussy Feels Like" and "Ablution." Fourteen pages of book reviews covered topics from anti-war to all versions of erotica. The middle section advertised such products as stationery which sported a personalized nude photo, a video entitled *Daddy and the Muscle Academy,* and several sexually oriented computer bulletin boards. There were a feast of specialty phone services, with names like "The Whip Line" and "The Venus Line," which was devoted to "Cross-Dressers and their Admirers." And, then, there came the pages of personal ads, some with revealing photos.

What distinguishes *EIDOS* from dozens of other sexually graphic periodicals is the philosophy of Brenda Tatelbaum, who self-consciously identifies with nineteenth-century free-love periodicals, such as *Lucifer, the Light Bearer.* The credo of *EIDOS* is spelled out in each issue:

> Our commitment to the Global Sex Village and the Global Grassroots Sexual Freedom Movement is based upon the following rationale: 1) To provide a forum, in the Thomas Jefferson tradition of a First Amendment 'wall of separation' for an international community of consenting adult individuals of all erotosexual orientations, preferences and lifestyles, who value their Sexual Freedom, Freedom of Sexual Self-Expression, Freedom of Personal Choice and Privacy Rights; 2) To advocate, ensure & promote the constitutional, civil and human rights of all Americans and global producers/consumers of erotica; 3) To encourage further growth of the erotic arts, sciences and

erotosexual lifestyles as a means to achieve an undisputed adult genre and standard of living.

From the start of our interview, Brenda laid the philosophical groundwork for her position. She objected to the word *pornography*, referring instead to *EIDOS* as "sexually explicit material written by and for adults." "Pornography," she insisted, "carries too much baggage." She sees *EIDOS* as documenting sexuality —the dark side, as well as the enlightened one.

EIDOS is an alternative to the slick, commercially motivated magazines like *Penthouse* and *Hustler*. It is the sort of publication that comes out because the people believe in sexual freedom so much they would operate at a loss, if necessary.

For Brenda, the commitment dates back to the early eighties, when she was writing erotic poetry and giving live readings. This was a period when women's study groups and periodicals were still talking about female eroticism and sexuality. Back then, she was putting out a publication that resembled a literary/art magazine on slick paper, with a color cover and little advertising. Nevertheless, it was attacked as smut. Brenda remarked, "No one in the community was upset with what I was doing; they were more upset that the police searched my home without a warrant." Ten years later, the atmosphere has changed, and Brenda doesn't believe people—especially feminists—would stand up publicly to defend her anymore. "It is as if all the sexual freedom that came before had never been."

Brenda knows that much of the new censorship comes from anti-porn feminists, whose "propaganda has been foisted on the public, especially the myth that crime and violence are related to sex."

I asked if she had ever been coerced into a pornographic act. "When I was married, of course, there were times when I didn't want to have sex. I agreed to when I didn't really want it, but that's basically it." Does she know of or has she heard of women being forced into sex acts by men using pornography? "I have never heard of such an incident. I have never been contacted by someone who conveyed such an incident to me. No."

I asked about S/M and bondage—activities that had been prominently displayed in the issues of *EIDOS* I'd read. "Is S/M more prone to violence than normal sex?" Brenda's reply was adamant. "The goal of S/M is to *not* go beyond the limits that have been set by the people involved," she assured me. "The scenario is laid out in advance; people know what to expect and there are certain code words that they use. If the code word is evoked, then that's that."

Brenda receives no support from feminists. This, despite the fact that she is a member of NOW and a pro-choice activist. It was when abortion rights came under attack by Reagan/Bush that Brenda first came into contact with the leaders of NOW in Boston. Many of the interactions were not pleasant. One day, a past president of the chapter stopped Brenda on the street; standing nose-to-nose, she looked Brenda in the eye and declared, "It is very difficult for me to take anything you do seriously." Brenda was stunned, "I thought to myself, 'Oh my God, what is this, out of nowhere.' I never spoke a word about it to anyone for years, but it kept crossing my mind."

Was this a typical reaction from NOW members? "NOW is quite happy to take my money, so I will be a member. But as far as my input on erotica . . . here, in the Boston area, they don't want me to be part of their workshops."

Brenda actively lectures on her own, but the circumstances are often skewed against her. Recently, for example, she was asked to speak on sexual freedom by the Women's Center at Northwestern University. The situation wasn't quite what Brenda had been led to expect. "I got there and they showed me a flier that had been posted on the wall. I hadn't realized that the night before Gail Dines of Wheelock College had been there in the same room presenting her slide show of pornography."

This is a slide show of tortured and mutilated women, often shown by anti-porn feminists as a prelude to a speech. Audiences naturally react with horrified indignation. The show is similar to the slides of mutilated fetuses that pro-lifers present, also as a prelude to discussion. Pro-choice advocates routinely denounce this tactic as unfair. They are not above adopting it, however, when it serves their own agenda.

The college paper *The Northeastern News* described this show: "She [Dines] cited *Hustler* magazine as a major contributor to the 'incredible holocaust against women going on today.' Dines showed the enthusiastic 50-member audience graphic photography of a staged pool-hall gang rape that appeared in that magazine . . . those photographs were tame in comparison to some of the others projected on the wall behind Dines. Other images featured women being tortured with ropes, pliers, vacuum cleaners, and high-heeled shoes."

Brenda had been given no indication that she was part of a two-night debate on pornography and violence. "I had prepared a speech, not a debate. . . . I thought about it and decided that I wasn't going to deal with their issues, but to address sexual freedom *as I had been asked to do.* I decided to establish the rich history of individualist feminist voices in abolitionism, suffrage, abortion . . . and how they were hounded by public opinion and censors. I went on for an hour and concluded that there really should be a course on the subject of sexual freedom."

In covering Brenda's presentation, the university paper reported, "She listed women's publications such as *On Our Backs* and *Taste of Latex* as examples from 'the wonderful world of sex-scene publishing.' Over 30 people were part of Tatelbaum's original audience, which dwindled to 11 by the end of her speech." The coverage ended by concluding that Brenda did not address the issues.

Brenda gave me her account. "The women in the audience

were angry because I totally ignored the issues of the night before. They didn't want to hear that there is a history of women suppressing women that no one knows about. No one challenged me, but some people—quite a few people—walked out."

Not surprisingly, Brenda believes that feminism's focus on politics is enslaving women sexually rather than empowering them; by denying sexuality, women lose their power. Brenda cited the Anita Hill sexual harassment case, during which now-Supreme Court Justice Clarence Thomas was accused of slipping a pubic hair into Hill's drink: "It is amazing to me that an Anita Hill—educated, successful, a beautiful woman—could be so devastated or brought down by a pubic hair put in her drink. What has happened to women's instincts for survival?"

Are things getting better or worse for sexual expression? Although Brenda expressed great relief at the Religious Right's no longer having such influence in the White House, she followed up with an interesting statement. "I did [Morton Downey's] show three times and when the show was eliminated—mostly by pressure from the left—that important forum for the alternative voice was gone."

In speculating on how the Religious Right (who view porn as sin) and the Radical Left (who view it as violence) are linking hands in a push for censorship, Brenda concluded with a question that has occurred to many of us, "Isn't it kind of bizarre to see the Left meeting up with the Right?"

KAT SUNLOVE

Kat Sunlove is the publisher and owner of the *Spectator*—California's Original Sex Newsmagazine. She describes herself as "a little Texas missionary." She adds, "When I was thirteen, I wanted to be a missionary to Russia and save the communists." Now she is a missionary for sexual freedom, especially for S/M, which "is so misunderstood."

I approached Kat through a mutual acquaintance in the industry, who vouched for me. Nevertheless, Kat wanted to know more about me. I immediately sent her several articles I had written on porn, scheduling our interview so that she would have time to look them over beforehand. Kat later explained her caution. Years ago, when she had a phone line as "Mistress Kat"— her persona in a column that advised S/M practitioners—she used to get threatening calls about how sick she was and how they were going to "get her." She has been cautious ever since.

I began by asking about an issue of the *Spectator* that I'd read. The July 22–28 issue featured "Samantha Strong Live at Kit Kat Club," the "Free Speech Coalition Awards," and "Stonewall 25 Snapshots." Clustered at the bottom and to the side of articles and personal ads were boxes that hawked a wide variety of phone-sex services—Chicks with Dicks, Slut Talk, Sexy She-Males, Clit-Lickin' Lesbians, to name a few. On page 7, respected feminist Pat Califia had a column called "Topping the News," which monitored efforts to suppress sexual information worldwide. On page 8, a "Public Services" section provided readers with phone numbers for suicide prevention and shelters for battered women.

"The *Spectator*," Kat informed me, "is an adult news magazine in tabloid format. It is an outgrowth of the old Berkeley *Barb*, which in the sixties was the mouthpiece for the free-speech movement on campus." The *Barb*—because it did not censor expression—tended to attract the fringes, the people whose lifestyles and opinions could find few other forums. Soon, the ad section was dominated by massage parlors, vendors of sex toys, and just ordinary people who were sexually adventurous. The *Barb* developed an extensive ad base of people with unusual sexual preferences.

Kat described the crisis this caused among the politically correct staff of the *Barb*. "As the MacKinnon philosophy started to take hold of the feminist circles—the flawed concept that somehow sexually oriented material led directly to violence toward women—the staff split and the *Barb* tried to find a comfortable place for everyone. They first put all the adult material into a center section. So you had this little irony of people riding on BART [San Francisco's transit system] supposedly reading the politic Berkeley *Barb* and really reading adult ads in the center section. Even that was not sufficient separation for the staff, so in '78 the two sections divided into two papers. The center section became the *Spectator*. In so doing, the *Barb* gave away its ad base and died within a year and a half."

The early *Spectator* tended to be a bit fluffy in its content: readers' fantasies and such. Kat was aware of this problem because, at the time, she was "Mistress Kat" writing an S/M advice column—"The Kat Box"—through which she became known as the Dear Abby of S/M. With a masters degree in political science, she brought a political orientation to her writing from the start. Then, in '87, the employees had a chance to buy the paper. As the *Spectator* changed hands, it became more political and unmistakably committed to free sexual expression.

I inquired into the political background Kat brought to the *Spectator*. "A strong sixties feminist background," she replied. She was one of the early members of NOW as well as of the Coalition of Labor Union Women. But now "I have a very hard time even using the term *feminist*. I really prefer the term *humanist*. I have been persuaded by the argument that if men went around calling themselves *masculists*, we would probably all be somewhat offended.

"If by *feminist* we mean someone who is devoted to the idea that the sexes should be equal in society, institutionally and every other way you can imagine, then I can wear that mantle very comfortably. But if there is another agenda underlying it, then I have some discomfort. I really believe that men have been—in quite different ways—equally oppressed by our society. They need as much help in getting to a state of equality. . . . Their inequalities come in the form of being the ones who get killed in war, who shoulder the financial burden. . . . The social expectations on them have been unkind in exactly mirror opposites."

How does she react to current feminist attacks on men, and on periodicals like the *Spectator*? "Well, I react first of all emotionally. Anger and irritation and sadness, because I feel they are so misled and so confused. Primarily, I'm insulted, because I'm an intelligent, independent, self-determined human being. And it is one of the reasons feminism originally appealed to me. It defined for me exactly what was in my heart and soul. I am insulted by the suggestion that I am incapable of making a choice around my life, lifestyle, sexuality, career, avocation, and entertainment. I can define these things for myself and have been doing so for a very long time, thank you very much."

Has she ever confronted such feminists? In the early eighties, when talk shows and other forums seemed to want to get information out, discussions were still possible. In the more recent years, however, debates tend to become circuses. Talk shows are now geared to controversy, not to understanding. As an example, Kat recalled a recent stint on the Jerry Springer show, where both she and anti-porn feminist Judith Reisman appeared as guests. Kat groaned, "The woman called me an adulteress on TV. I thought—'Get a grip, lady, I'm not even married.'" During a break, Judith pointedly informed Kat, who was trying to open a conversation, "I'm not here to have a dialogue with you."

Any real discussions she's had on porn have occurred at meetings, such as NOW conferences. Recently, however, Kat has felt alienated from those NOW members, who seem determined to identify as victims. At a recent San Francisco NOW conference, Kat got so irate at a panel on sexual harassment that she almost walked out. Remember that, in '94, NOW joined in accusing an L.A. fireman of sexual harassment because he read a *Playboy* on his own time. At the panel, women in the audience kept standing up to say how intimidated or degraded they would have felt by the fireman's reading habits. "I can't cope with that." Kat recoiled from the women who seemed to be embracing weakness. "Women have a lot of power sexually. It's supply and demand. We definitely have something that men want very badly."

Had she ever experienced the sort of intimidation the panel discussed? Had she ever been coerced into a pornographic act? "Most certainly not. Quite the contrary. My persona as 'Mistress Kat' allows me courtesies from producers and theater owners."

Did she know of anyone who was coerced? "People approach things with different baggage and strengths. I would say that most of what I witnessed that struck me as 'coerced' was because of a weak personality. You know, a lack of self-esteem that came much earlier, not something you could track to the industry. This is not a good industry for some people to be in, just as stock-brokering may not be a good job for those with weak nerves." I made it clear that by *coercion* I meant "physical force." "I have never even heard a report that someone was physically abused." Nor had she ever seen a snuff movie, or known anyone who had.

What about the mock violence in porn? How realistic is it? Although a lot of videos in seventies had mock rape scenes, when the line that "porn leads to violence" started to gain acceptance, the industry said, "We won't mix anything remotely like that with hard-core porn."

Like most other aspects of porn, the *Spectator* is caught up in self-censorship. Some of the self-restraint comes from Kat's personal values—for example, there are no children or animals represented because "they are unable to consent." Most of the censorship, however, comes from the need to comply with anti-porn laws, such as AB17. This California law requires news racks on the street that contain "harmful" material to be constantly supervised by an adult to assure that minors have no access to it. Since such monitoring would be prohibitively expensive, the law essentially bars "harmful" material from distribution. The *Spectator* avoids being so labeled by eschewing hard-core material, such as vaginal penetration or fully erect cocks. Even if the sex is simulated, but looks real, Kat asks for an alternative shot. She is trying to be what she calls "a good neighbor."

Nevertheless, the *Spectator* experiences ongoing harassment from legal challenges to its right to distribute. For example, as we spoke, Kat received a note telling her to call the San Carlos planning commission about a local ordinance on news racks.

The *Spectator* is particularly vulnerable to such ordinances, because it is one of the last accessible forums for the discussion of S/M, which has few defenders. Why? "If you haven't had the experience of enjoying S/M, it may look silly or like violence. If you have had the enjoyment, it looks like erotica because you know what is happening, what the people are feeling and thinking. It has its own rules." If you take S/M at face value, as though the behavior was taking place spontaneously in your own living room, then the scene might well be degrading and frightening. The point is that S/M is game-playing. Far from being spontaneous, everything is discussed and agreed-upon in advance.

So, how did a self-described "little Texas missionary" get to be the Dear Abby of sadomasochism? She was lovingly seduced to it by a male friend she had known for four years and, so, trusted. She started by being submissive to her partner and then, "I turned the tables on him a few months later and became the dominant one." Both experiences were valuable. "During my submissive period, I reowned a part of myself that is precious and that through my upbringing in this society and my adoption of feminism, I had abandoned, I had disowned. A loving, submissive person. . . . On the other hand, being a dominant and getting comfortable with power has helped me become a good publisher who makes the company grow."

As a woman to whom S/M has seemed very strange, I wanted to know what attracted her to it. "The joy of S/M is to trust your partner and relax, to flow like a leaf on a sexual river. You know you are basically safe, but there is the thrill of danger, as on a roller coaster or in sky diving. There is an energy exchange . . .

almost a telepathic connection takes place. It is a magical thing. S/M has to do with the side of human nature that we do not like to look at."

Is real pain involved? Yes and no. "If you burn your tongue on a cup of coffee, it hurts. If your lover threatens you with a match close to your lips, you are going to feel a thrill in your tongue, I guarantee it. The erotic component changes it from violence to something that is exciting."

She just wishes it were possible to talk more freely about S/M and to have a real dialogue with its critics. But they have made it clear that discussion with women like her is not welcome.

CONCLUSION

As a feminist who has taken the trouble to do empirical research —to look the porn industry in the eye—I have come to several conclusions:

1. Although amateur porn may contain scenes of real violence, I have not found even convincing scenes of mock violence in the pornography put out by the industry today.

2. To the extent that sex workers are battered, it seems to result from being denied the protection of law and legitimacy. Whenever porn is allowed to emerge from the underground, even into the shadows, the working conditions of the women improve tremendously. And they are safer.

3. I like the women. As in every industry, some women in porn are undoubtedly damaged by the choices they are making. But the women I encountered were not victims. They were rebellious, a bit raunchy, shrewd at business, and they didn't take shit from anyone.

4. All of the willingness to openly discuss women's sexuality seems to come from the pro-pornography side. The women in

porn seem unwilling to denounce the sexual attitudes of others—even of feminists who were trying to silence them.

5. The most interesting work on women's sexuality is coming from the women in porn who are pushing through all the barriers to produce, direct, and own their own companies.

6. On a strictly personal level—the porn I viewed and the women I interviewed provoked some strange reactions in me, uncomfortable reactions. For example, I felt threatened by a prostitute's fervid arguments that no man—not a single one—was capable of monogamy. It would have been easy for me to translate my discomfort into a dislike of the woman who was "causing" it. It would have been easier to blame her than to dwell on my own insecurities.

Perhaps this is why society reviles sex workers. Perhaps they show us things we don't want to see.

EIGHT

WHITHER PORNOGRAPHY?

A main theme of this book is that pornography is a business like any other. It offers women rewards and insults, profits and losses. As an industry, pornography may be rawer and less self-regulating than many others. This is probably because—unlike insurance or advertising—it has only been legal for some twenty years.

Pornography needs to catch up with the changes in attitude that have swept the "outside" world. It needs to begin treating women with more respect, on at least two levels: Women who work in pornography should have better working conditions, including contracts and access to positions of power; and, women who constitute a huge and growing market for pornography should be taken seriously as consumers.

WOMEN IN THE INDUSTRY

Women who work in pornography should have better working conditions, including contracts and access to positions of power. Women in pornography have less control over their working conditions than most women do. There are several reasons for this. One of them is that women often work without contracts.

If feminists are concerned with the well-being of women in pornography, they should pressure the industry to institute protections for women.

If feminists wish to protect women in pornography, if they truly care, they must open up a dialogue with those who can exercise influence and control. Pornographers are businessmen and businesswomen, like any others. They respond to customer feedback and social pressure. So far, feminists have been speaking mostly to themselves. They have blithely assumed pornographers would never listen to their point of view. I have found the opposite to be true.

How can feminists claim that the porn industry is unreceptive to their points of view? How many feminists have taken the effort to make an approach?

The following is an edited version of an article I published in *Adult Video News* (AVN), which is the main trade journal of pornography. It is part of my commitment to influence the industry toward treating women better.

AVN not only accepted the following article; the editor with whom I worked, Mark Kearnes, was among the most pleasant I've encountered. The magazine circulated the piece to men in the industry and elicited their comments, which were printed as sidebars. Then, the *Spectator*, California's Original Sex Newsmagazine, requested permission to reprint the article.

"How can the porn industry protect itself? First and foremost: contracts. The issue confronting the industry in the nineties will be violence against women and coercion of women, and producers of XXX tapes may well be called upon to produce contracts to protect themselves against these very charges; that is, the charge that a woman did not give true or informed consent to pose or perform. To be effective, these contracts should be executed before, not after, the shooting; they should be witnessed by two parties (who may be other actors, stage hands, even the director himself); they must explicitly state the scope of sexual activities being agreed to and the purpose of the performance, namely to produce sexually explicit material for distribution. In addition, the contract should explicitly name all the rights—national/international distribution, use of, etc.—transferred to the producer. The document should also specify remedies for breach of contract on either side (e.g., binding arbitration to resolve differences). Each and every contract should include the standard model release and photocopied documentation of the actress's age.

"Among Hollywood types, and anyone else who deals regularly with contracts, this may seem to be nothing more than common sense, but a woman being put under contract is actually news in the porn industry. In a sense, the industry's way of dealing with the makers of XXX material is patterned by its years-gone tradition of functioning outside the judiciary, and the suspicion (sometimes justified) that the police and the court system can be expected to be either hostile or irrelevant to internecine industry concerns. The whole way of doing business is reminiscent of Bob Dylan's line, 'To live outside the law you must be honest.' But the days of ignoring the niceties of paperwork are over; today's carefully worded contract may be the only defense against a lawsuit two years down the line.

"Yet producers remain almost criminally naive about the need to document informed consent. After criticizing producer John Stagliano in person about not signing contracts with his actresses, I followed up with a phone call. When I harped upon this theme, the generally affable Stagliano snapped back, 'I borrowed some forms. I'm getting contracts, okay?'

"I hope to similarly irritate other directors/producers into operating only on the basis of signed contracts.

"As an outsider looking in, I would suggest two steps the XXX industry could take to protect itself from the growing threat of lawsuits. First, lawyers involved in the Free Speech Coalition, or some other trade organization, could produce a model contract which would emphasize informed consent, detail the transfer of rights, and set forth the forum for remedies in case of a breach by either side. This contract would be made available as a standard for the industry. For a nominal yearly fee, the law firm drawing the contract, or the Free Speech Coalition, or some other organization or individual, could take on the job of registering signed contracts, so that the parties could assure themselves that they are dealing with companies that would be unlikely to involve them in a messy lawsuit. Registering the contracts would also preserve a record of agreements.

"Certainly, there is a legitimate concern in the industry about 'paper trails,' and contracts would, after all, constitute business records easily traceable to a finished product—a product which might be busted in any jurisdiction around the country. However, the type of contract involved here would bear no relation to an obscenity bust, since the finished tape is what's under question, not whether the actors were paid to perform; their performance in the feature is a given— though a contract would establish that the performance wasn't coerced. Second, a trade organization should establish procedures by which the industry can

regulate itself against genuine abuses, such as refusal to
pay on a contract, or last-minute cancellation of a
shoot. Most industries and professions have some
method of regulating themselves. Lawyers have the
Bar Association. Doctors have the AMA. Writers have
the Guild. Although these trade associations often do
not carry the force of law—or even of licensing—
they do wield great power in terms of exposing and
publically censuring abuses. Obviously, few of the
XXX industry have any wish to 'air their dirty laun-
dry in public,' but peer pressure alone can cure many
situations. More extreme tactics, like boycotts by performers of a director or a company, are always available.

"The conflict between the politically correct and
those who wish access to sexually explicit material is
irreconcilable and, perhaps, inevitable. In this battle,
pornography occupies the moral high ground, because
it defends the right of a woman to choose her own lifestyle. The porn industry should rush to do its part by
making women's choices explicit—in contracts and in
establishing procedures that protect women from
abuse by unethical producers."

WOMEN WHO CONSUME PORNOGRAPHY

*Women, who constitute a huge and growing market for
pornography, should be taken seriously as consumers.*
Pornography is like any other business: It is out to make money.
This means that producers and distributors listen to the feedback
they receive from customers. Here, the much maligned profit
motive can work to the advantage of women. The producers who
heed their customers' voices will prosper. In doing so, they will

also introduce new and higher employment standards throughout the industry.

In talking to producers and distributors, I have found them to be not only open to feminist ideas, but eager to hear them. At one point, I had to refuse a rather persistent offer to consult on a porn shoot. The Young Turk producer wanted a feminist slant on some of the scenes of his video-in-progress. Fortunately, I was able to plead that such an arrangement might bring my objectivity into question. I say "fortunately" because I found the prospect of watching real people having real sex oddly disturbing. Instead, I offered to review the finished product on an informal (nonfinancial) basis.

My point is: The industry responds to feedback. Feminists are missing a glistening opportunity to provide real protection for women.

The message of this book is *not* that every woman should read or watch pornography. It is that every woman should decide for herself.

Making an informed decision requires knowledge. The following is a brief list of companies and organizations that offer information on pornography, whether as a political pursuit or for pleasure.

PORNOGRAPHY AS POLITICS
The following organizations will give a glimpse of what is out there to those of you who wish to become politically active on behalf of pornography.

Feminists for Free Expression
Executive Director, Rachel Hickerson
2525 Times Square Station
New York, New York 10108-2525
(212) 496-8356 FAX (212) 787-5285

Organized to fight censorship, the Board of FFE reads like a feminist honor list. Members include Nadine Strossen, Betty Friedan, Nancy Friday, and Erica Jong.

COYOTE (Call Off Your Old Tired Ethics)
Director, Norma Jean Almodovar
1626 North Wilcox, #580
Hollywood, CA 90028
(818) 892-1859

COYOTE (San Francisco)
2269 Chestnut Street, #452
San Francisco, CA 94123
(415) 435-7950

COYOTE is the only national sex worker's advocacy group in America. Although it is geared toward women in sex work, those who wish to speak out for sexual freedom are welcome to join.

CAL-ACT (Californians Act Against Censorship Together)
Bobby Lilly, Editor
2550 Shattuck Avenue, #51
Berkeley, CA 94704
(510) 548-3695

The slogan on CAL-ACT's masthead is "Defending our right to freedom of expression, especially sexual expression." An activist organization, CAL-ACT fights for free sexual expression in California, a state in which it seems to be under particular attack.

Free Speech Coalition
22968 Victory Boulevard, Suite 248
Woodland Hills, CA 91367
(818) 348-9373 or (800) 845-8503

This organization represents and provides legal advice for the pornography industry.

American Civil Liberties Union
National Headquarters
132 West 43rd Street
New York, New York 10036
(212) 944-9800 or FAX (212) 345-5290

Although the ACLU is still the loudest voice in support of the First Amendment, internal conflicts over the issues of sexual harassment and pornography threaten to dull the organization's free-speech fervor. Those who join now have a chance to influence its direction, especially while Nadine Strossen—a one-woman crusade for freedom of speech—is president.

PORNOGRAPHY AS PLEASURE
This list is not an endorsement of the following companies. Since everything in pornography is a matter of preference, I merely offer a broad spectrum.

Femme Productions
588 Broadway, Suite 1100
New York, New York 10012
(212) 226-9330

Owned by the iconoclastic Candida Royalle, Femme Productions produces high-quality, well-scripted pornography that is aimed at "the woman who knows what she wants and the men who love her."

Adam and Eve
Apple Court, P.O. Box 400
Carrboro, North Carolina 27510
(919) 929-2143

The largest distributor of adult videos in America, Adam and Eve also sends out regular catalogs that advertise a wide range of sexual toys and specialty items. It gives a good indication of what is available in the mainstream.

Vivid Video
15127 Califa Street
Van Nuys, California 91411
(818) 908-0481

One of the best mainstream producers of both hard- and soft-core pornography. Although Vivid does not put the time and budget into their films that Femme does, neither do they charge as much for their product.

Adult Video News/subscription
8600 West Chester Pike, Suite 300
Upper Darby, PA 19082
(215) 789-2085

Well-written and glossy, this is pornography's trade publication. Each month, it lists and reviews current video releases, as well as monitors the political/legal scene as it affects the industry.

Spectator
Editor, Kat Sunlove
P.O. Box 1984
Berkeley, CA 94701
(510) 849-1615

Self-described as "California's Weekly Sex Newsmagazine," the Spectator emphasizes bondage and dominance, and features an extensive personal ads section.

EIDOS (Everyone Is Doing Outrageous Sex)
Editor, Brenda Loew Tatelbaum
P.O. Box 96
Boston, MA 02137-0096
(617) 262-0096 FAX (617) 364-0096

This is a sexually explicit feminist tabloid, which combines graphic photos with erotic fiction, book reviews, and political insight.

Enjoy!

NINE

A COYOTE MEETING

After the Consumer Electronics Show, I spent several days in Los Angeles, during which I attended a meeting of COYOTE (Call Off Your Old Tired Ethics), the only national sex worker's rights organization. It was established by Margo St. James in 1972 as a prostitute's advocacy group. COYOTE soon expanded its political scope to represent the interests of all sex workers. As Executive Director Norma Jean Almodovar explained, "We realized we were all in it together."

Pornography and prostitution have a great deal in common: They both involve sex for money and they share the same enemies. It has long been argued that pornography is a form of prostitution. The only difference between the two acts is that a camera is running while the porn act is being performed.

The debate is heating up on whether being paid to perform a legal act (that is, to have sex) should be illegal. At one extreme of the debate, ex-porn queen "Holly Ryder," aka Lisa Marie Abato, is crusading to collect one million signatures to put an initiative on the 1994 California state ballot to change the state constitution so as to prohibit the production of pornography in California.

At the other extreme, actress Roseanne Arnold openly admitted to *Vanity Fair* that she had briefly worked as a prostitute. In her own words, "I think prostitution should be legal, because the way any society treats prostitutes reflects directly on how it treats the highest and most powerful woman."[1]

It is no coincidence that this debate is taking place in Los Angeles, where eighty percent of the country's sexually explicit films are made.

It is in Los Angeles that COYOTE is being rebuilt. COYOTE—Call Off Your Old Tired Ethics—is the nation's loudest voice for the rights of sex workers. It has been strangely quiet in the last few years, but this is beginning to change. The Executive Director is now Norma Jean Almodovar, who also heads the influential Los Angeles chapter. Ms. Almodovar, who spent eighteen months in a California state prison on pandering charges, is the author of *From Cop to Call Girl.* With prison behind her, she is concentrating her efforts on COYOTE and on writing a book about her prison experience.

Only sex workers or their advocates are invited to COYOTE meetings—and an invitation is necessary to attend. Since I qualified on the latter count, I found myself—at two p.m. on a bright Sunday afternoon—standing outside an upscale condominium, asking to be buzzed in.

Again, I dressed in feminist drag: Reeboks, blue jeans, and a loose sweater. But, this time, it was for an entirely different reason. Instead of wanting to set myself apart, I wanted to blend into the group. It was Sunday; Norma Jean had assured me the meeting was casual; I didn't want to look like an outsider.

Norma Jean's husband met me at the door with a welcoming smile. Norma Jean stood in the kitchen, wearing a pale blue jeans outfit with a design in metal studs across the top. She was presiding over the preparation of a feast consisting of huge trays of chicken wings, egg rolls, pizza snacks, lasagna, meat balls, garlic bread, and potato chips. "The leftovers from a Christmas party," she explained, sticking the name tag "Wendy" on my chest and handing me a plate, with exhortations to "eat!"

(Later in the business portion of the meeting she asked for a volunteer to assume food duty for upcoming meetings. A small blonde—in sneakers, blue jeans, and a loose sweater—agreed to phone COYOTE members to coordinate casseroles and snacks. It all seemed so normal, like a church choir meeting I once attended.)

With a full plate of lasagna and chicken wings, I scoped out the living room. Over a dozen people—three of them men—were sprawled across the two couches, various chairs, and the floor. I sized up the group. The women all wore jeans or slacks, with T-shirts or some type of sweater. Only one or two seemed to be wearing make-up, and none of them had their hair "fixed" in anything but a ponytail. There was an Asian woman, but no other discernible minorities. Except for a woman in her fifties, the average age was about thirty. One of the three men was dressed in a suit; the other two were casual.

I tried to judge from their faces and attitudes as to who they were—sex worker or sexual rights advocate? Was the thirtyish tired-looking woman—the only one to wear heavy makeup—a prostitute? The older woman, who smiled up pleasantly from the floor, did she work a sex phone line? What about the pumped-up young guy, was he a male stripper? And how did they peg me?

At the right end of a large wooden coffee table, an attractive, angry-looking woman sat cross-legged, while an intense-looking man hovered. He placed two sheets of paper in front of her and gestured toward them as he spoke.

I caught the gist of the exchange. His name was Edward Tabash, a Beverly Hills lawyer whose passion was civil liberties. One of the sheets of paper was a photocopy of an op-ed by him from the *Los Angeles Times* entitled "Stop Jailing Women for

Their Own Good," with the subtitle, "Prostitution: Forbidding sale of sex by consenting adults is paternalistic and condescending." The editorial read, in part:

> The paternalistic argument . . . claims that in order to protect women against such exploitation, society should imprison all women who engage in prostitution. This argument is reducible to a claim that languishing behind bars is a preferable fate for a woman as opposed to allowing her to freely sell her body. . . .[2]

The other sheet gave the details of a recent court decision on entrapment. No longer would a police officer who slept with a prostitute be able to testify in court against her, since he was now considered to be an accomplice to the crime.

I asked if they minded my joining the conversation. The woman seemed annoyed—what I later discovered was her pervasive attitude toward everything—and Tabash seemed "professional." He went into the same patter with me as with the other woman. I wondered whether he consciously distanced himself from women "in the business" or whether he was just being careful around someone he didn't know.

The conversation ended and another sprang up. The woman who had smiled pleasantly announced that this was her first time at a COYOTE meeting. She didn't know what to expect. The heavily made-up woman piped in with the same information. I relaxed as I realized that COYOTE was probably more intimidating to sex workers than it was to me. After all, I was used to standing up for myself.

Our chat was cut short by an odd coincidence. The distant acquaintance whom I had met at CES walked through the door, jumped a few inches at the sight of me, then gravitated to where I was sitting. It was his first COYOTE meeting as well, and I began to appreciate how the organization was just now rebuilding itself.

D. and I fell into an easy conversation about old times until I noticed that several people—including Tabash—were listening to us. I realized how no one else seemed to be talking to each other as D. and I were—that is, on a personal level. No one was asking the typical "new person" questions like, What do you do for a living? Are you married? How long have you lived in L.A.? Where do you come from originally?

Norma Jean signaled an abrupt end to all conversation by calling the meeting to order. The living room now held about thirty people, one of whom was the guest speaker, attorney Tom Tanana.

A series of papers was passed from person to person and when they got around to me I found they included a COYOTE memo with the meeting's business agenda, Tabash's op-ed piece, and an update on the crusade of "Holly Ryder." The first order of business was the same disclaimer that appeared at the top of the COYOTE memo:

> We hereby exercise our constitutional right to assemble peaceably for the purpose of engaging in political activity. It is our belief that the laws of the state of California which prohibit adult commercial sexual activity violate the right to privacy and are therefore unconstitutional and we seek to have those laws overturned. We assert our right to assemble without the intrusion of any government agent(s) acting in a covert undercover manner in our meetings.
>
> All attendees are free to exchange personal information for the purpose of furthering our political goals. All conduct that is currently prohibited by law is forbidden at any COYOTE sponsored function, and no implied consent is given by *any* COYOTE

member . . . to engage in any activity that is illegal. Please do not place any of us in jeopardy by engaging in any illegal activity during this meeting. Thank you.

Norma Jean repeated this disclaimer and, so, distanced herself from conducting a meeting to facilitate prostitution, which could have resulted in a pandering charge. She said everyone could use their own names or pseudonyms, as they wished. Tanana's talk would be recorded, but if anyone did not want his or her voice to be on tape the recorder would be stopped and the question repeated on tape by Tanana before he answered it. After Norma Jean finished, Tabash re-emphasized that the First Amendment guaranteed the right to assemble for political purposes. Both of them were covering every base, in case an undercover agent happened to be present.

The business meeting began. Norma Jean gave an overview of current COYOTE activities, which included contacting Roseanne Arnold and inviting her to join the organization. A similar invitation had been made to actor John Larroquette, whose weekly television show features a prostitute who is witty, in control, and very human.

Tabash's op-ed piece was held up, followed by another article from the *Los Angeles Times*, which discussed a woman who offered free self-help classes to current or former prostitutes. Norma Jean asserted, "I feel proud of what I did when I was a prostitute, but in case *you* don't . . ." She read the information aloud and left the news clipping on a table by the front door.

Next, the group coordinated a March 2nd trip to San Francisco in order to meet with COYOTE members up there. The main topic for discussion between the two memberships was whether COYOTE should push to legalize prostitution or to decriminalize it. Norma Jean wants decriminalization, since legalization would entail the same hardships that women experience in Nevada. There, prostitutes are treated like civil servants; they clock into government-licensed brothels where working conditions have all the charm of a post office. They have no selection in clients, no control over what they charge or the hours they work. (A major attraction of prostitution, especially to women with children, are the flexible hours and independence.)

Legalized prostitutes have to "register" with the police, and so lose the anonymity that permits them to move easily out of the profession into marriage or other employment. Moreover, the women have to obey a slate of laws that apply only to them. For example, they are not supposed to be on the streets at night, even to walk to the corner store for a quart of milk for their kids' cereal in the morning. They do not enjoy the same freedom as every other woman in Nevada.

Decriminalization, on the other hand, merely defines prostitution as an activity that is not addressed by the law. Being a prostitute would be no more regulated than being a secretary.

A sign-up sheet for the trip to San Francisco was passed around, and I was amazed by how many people signed up— including D. After all, they had to pay for their own ticket and take time away from work and family. The group might be fairly new, but a hard core was developing fast.

The featured speaker, who was from San Diego, began by commenting on how police were cracking down on prostitution there and asked what the situation was in L.A. Two women claimed things were even worse in L.A.

Tanana's talk centered around entrapment laws, the laws by which a policeman poses as a trick and lures a prostitute into solicitation. Changes in the law appear to be weighed in favor of the prostitute because the current wording requires her to give a "manifestation of consent" to any offer of money for sex. But, as Norma Jean observed and as the lawyers confirmed, "manifestation" can mean a nod, a smile, a shrug of the shoulders, or even a suggestive silence. Moreover, if the policeman decides to lie, no court or jury would believe a whore over a cop.

Tom advised that entrapment should be a defense of last resort, since the prostitute has to admit guilt and then plead extenuating circumstances. He also painted a bleak picture for the possibility of avoiding entrapment.

"What if I ask the guy if he's a cop?" asked a striking redhead with granny glasses and a steno pad.

"He can deny it and still make the charges stick," Tabash replied.

"What if I'm careful?" the irritated brunette to my right interjected. "What if I just say . . ." her voice sank to a whisper that went with a seductive shifting of her shoulders, "hey, do you want to party? Or, I could carry a recorder in my purse and tape the whole thing."

"The police would throw the tape away," Tanana answered.

"If you make trouble and you have children, they could threaten to take them away," added Tabash.

"They *would* threaten to take them away!" corrected the redhead, and quoted the section of law under which the authorities could do it.

Tanana offered a piece of advice, "Something I've seen work if you think the policeman is taping you, is to say out-of-the-blue, 'Don't touch me there!' It makes the cop look bad and the tape is hard to use against you."

As "what can be done" became the center of discussion, people began to share their stories. The man in the suit, P., sitting directly behind me, spoke up. He had owned a successful escort service until—as he put it—certain "competitors" wanted him out of the business. The police tapped his phone on their own initiative and found out where and when to expect his escorts. Eventually, they were able to arrest him.

"But a phone tap like that wouldn't be admissible as evidence in court," D. insisted.

Tom agreed. Illegal taps were not admissible evidence, but they were nevertheless constantly used to convict people. Example: If the police suspect someone of holding up liquor stores, they can bug his phone and find out when and where the next robbery is planned. Then, a police car can arrange to be across the street from that store at the proper time. The phone tap need never come up in court. The same is true with prostitution. As well, the police can use phone recordings to intimidate the women.

Tanana urged everyone to be careful on the phone and to tape their own conversations so they could prove what had really been said. The Asian woman objected, "If I have nothing to hide, why should I bother to tape myself?" Both lawyers answered in unison, "Self-defense."

In order to illustrate the dangers, Tanana went into his own experiences with police in San Diego, where he walks the city's equivalent of a strip and passes out fliers telling women where to go for legal aid and how to report police abuse. Not long ago, women on the strip began warning him that a particular policeman intended to pick him up and "beat the shit out of him."

He encountered the officer and they had words, during which the policeman refused to give Tanana his badge number. Later in the evening, Tanana tried to cross an empty street at a marked crosswalk. The only car in sight—a police car—drove up and cut him off. Tanana asked the officer to move and was informed that he was "interfering with a police investigation." He was issued a first warning.

Turning around, Tanana realized that in order to cross the street legally and get to his car, he would have to go through other policemen who were standing at the curbs. Every legal route to his car involved encountering policemen. He asked the officer in the patrol car, "How can I get back to my car without interfering with a police investigation a second time?"

The officer responded, "You're an adult. Figure it out."

Tanana changed tactics. "Then, can you tell me the scope of the police investigation so that I can be sure to stay out of it?"

The officer responded, "You're an adult. Figure it out."

What finally saved Tanana was the video camera with which many police vehicles are now equipped. The video would have shown the "set-up," but—somehow—before Internal Affairs could act on it, the tape was lost and the matter was dropped. According to Tom, he lives in fear of drugs being planted on him.

"What can be done?" became the heated question. A strategy was suggested: Whenever a woman was arrested for solicitation, she should insist on her right to an immediate jury trial. This would clog the system to the point of breakdown. Tabash seemed to disagree. For one thing, a lot of courts like those in Santa Monica were not backlogged. For another thing, women who demanded jury trials or caused other difficulties were bound to receive much stiffer sentences and fines than if they just pleaded guilty. An attorney, he argued, has to represent the interests of a specific client. He would have to advise against such a course of action.

Norma Jean suggested a useful way to psychologically approach policemen and courts. She observed that the current laws against prostitution were ostensibly there to protect women in the business. Many feminists and lawmakers actually believed that prostitutes were psychologically damaged and incapable of choosing what they did. She urged the women to refuse to let anyone treat them like mental incompetents. If they insisted on their rights and on their competence to choose, it would give them the psychological advantage.

Meanwhile, people continued to arrive. As they announced their names over the apartment intercom, Norma Jean checked that the newcomers were known and had been invited by someone in the group before buzzing them in. I discreetly caught Norma Jean's attention and told her the name of a friend who would be arriving shortly to drive me to another meeting.

I had hardly passed this news on when my friend showed up. I hurried her into the seclusion of the kitchen. There, I discreetly exchanged information with P., whose case interested me. Always a quick study, my friend stayed to one side, chewing on chicken wings. She scanned the handout that spelled out the business agenda. The section "Future Topics for Speakers" seemed to catch her attention.

1. Plastic Surgery—how to prolong our looks for the biz
2. Sex Surrogacy—how to make the transition
3. Bail Bondsmen—how to find one who will be on call
4. Legit Massage—how to enter, get training, etc.
5. Tax Planning—investments and how to get credit
6. How to Win a Claim Against a Bad-Check Client

Oddly enough, the thing that has haunted me about the COYOTE meeting was not the speaker or the audience. It was a comment my friend made.

When we were settled in her car, she turned and asked with genuine concern, "Are you all right?" The question caught me off guard. I wanted to know why she asked. "Because your face is beet-red and it has been that way for the last ten minutes." A glance in the rearview mirror confirmed this. I suddenly realized how angry I was. How angry I had become over the last few hours while listening to how society treated prostitutes like dirt because it didn't like their sexual choices.

I wondered if feminists who attack prostitutes as psychological incompetents had ever met women in the industry—not the victims who flee, but the majority who stay. I wondered if I could ever again blithely exhort sex workers to "stand up for yourself" when I now knew they could lose their children for following my advice. How many times through history have women had to defend themselves against self-proclaimed "protectors"? By defining myself as an advocate of sex worker's rights—a protector—wasn't I placing myself on a higher level than these "unfortunate" women?

Maybe sex workers are like every other type of women in our society. Maybe they just need a bit of respect. It's a lesson I'm still learning.

Appendix

COYOTE Survey

In trying to get a better portrait of women in pornography—
many of whom have done other sex work, such as stripping or
telephone sex work—I arranged to survey the COYOTE membership. (A sample, blank survey appears on pages 226–228.) One
thing I wanted to see was whether surveys from women who
worked in pornography differed substantially from those returned by women who were, for example, prostitutes.

About two hundred four-page questionnaires were distributed by various COYOTE chapters to their memberships
across North America; I received forty-one responses back in the
mail. (Note: Since answering any specific question was optional,
not all questions received forty-one answers.) The surveys contained invaluable information from generous women who took
the time not only to answer my questions carefully, but also to
enclose extra sheets of paper describing everything from one
prostitute's brutal run-in with the police to another woman's
battle to have her daughter play on a Little League baseball team
which discriminated against girls.

The most surprising thing to me was that not a single woman

who responded worked in pornography. Not one of the women indicated having *ever* worked in porn in answering the questions: How did you enter sex work? or What jobs have you held? The breakdown of respondents was: 30 prostitutes, 6 masseuses, 5 strippers, 4 dominatrixes, 3 madams, 2 phone sex workers, 1 mud wrestler, and 1 ambiguous survey where the woman defined her job as "providing a sex-positive environment." (Answers total more than forty-one due to multiple responses.)

I can only speculate as to why COYOTE, as an organization for sex workers' rights, does not attract women in porn. After all, the head of COYOTE in California, Norma Jean Almodovar, is well known and well liked in the industry, although she has never worked in porn. A primary reason may be that, since pornography is legal, women in the industry do not feel the same urgent need to assert their rights as prostitutes do. Yet this does not explain why women who strip and do phone sex—also legal activities—join COYOTE.

Perhaps alternative organizations within pornography, such as the Free Speech Association, absorb the women who are politically inclined. Perhaps the industry's drift toward respectability has made it reluctant to align with less socially accepted forms of sex work. Or COYOTE may have done little outreach among porn actresses, who are well-treated compared to many other sex workers.

Even without the presence of women in porn, I decided to include a brief overview of the COYOTE survey for three reasons:

1. The accusations hurled at porn actresses are basically the same charges brought against all female sex workers—eg., they are coerced, they are psychologically damaged, they are pathetic drug-abusing victims. If these accusations are proven false about sex workers in general, then there is reason to doubt their validity about women in pornography in particular.

2. If female sex workers are victims, you would expect this to be particularly true of women who are involved in illegal sex work (e.g., prostitutes). After all, those involved in legal sex work (porn actresses) have far greater protection from the law and from the greater acceptance of society. If prostitutes are shown to be independent women, rather than victims, this should hold true to an even greater degree for women in porn.

3. There is no hard-and-fast distinction between prostitution and pornography, which has been called "prostitution in front of a camera." Numerous district attorneys have redefined the two "crimes" in order to fold them into one. In the recent attack on the industry, former porn actress Holly Ryder and her Los Angeles–based political action committee wanted to redefine women in pornography as prostitutes under the California state constitution. Ms. Ryder's initiative read: "Prostitution includes acts of sexual intercourse or sodomy for money or other consideration, for . . . the purpose of observation by persons present during the act or persons absent during the act observing by means of visual recording or broadcast; and the right to perform acts of prostitution shall be denied . . ."

Prostitution and pornography share characteristics: They both involve sex for money; society shuns them both; laws that repress one have historically rebounded on the other; and, the attitudes of the women within the two professions sometimes seem remarkably similar. For this reason, a survey involving prostitutes gives perspective on women in pornography.

I want to begin by stating the survey's limitations.

It is an informal survey, not a controlled study. Such a survey, especially one limited to forty-one respondents, proves nothing. But it can *dis*prove a great deal. This harkens back to first-year logic class. There, students learn to disprove the statement "All swans are white" by finding just one black swan. Accordingly, to disprove the anti–sex worker claim that "Prostitutes are drug abusers or victims of incest," all you need to do is find one prostitute who does not fall into those categories. This invalidates those claims.

Moreover, although the data in this survey may *prove* nothing, it does indicate possible directions for promising research. For example, in answer to the question "At what age did you enter sex work?", both the mean and the median answer was "At twenty-seven years old." Four women (10%) began sex work in their teens; twenty-one women (51%) entered in their twenties; thirteen women (32%) began in their thirties; three women (7%) in their forties. The most common answer was "At twenty years old." This may well indicate that most women who enter sex work are adults, well past the age of consent and self-determination. The two women who began sex work at forty-two are particularly intriguing, because they break several cultural stereotypes.

Another caveat about the survey: All the women surveyed belong to COYOTE, an outspoken political rights organization. This means that the sampling is not random. These are socially aware women, who are successful enough at their chosen careers to have time for political agitation. This places them well above the level of streetwalkers—women who are often preoccupied with sheer survival, women for whom there is no effective advocacy organization.

The respondents are also willing to be visible, as evidenced by how many of them provided me with their phone numbers and/or addresses. Visibility brings vulnerability. This may account for how few of the women (only 20%) reported having children. Authorities often intimidate sex workers by threatening to take away their children. Thus, the survey is skewed in favor of sex workers who feel less vulnerable—that is, who do not have children. There may well be other hidden biases.

Nevertheless, the survey represents an empirical and pioneering examination of whether or not women sex workers consent to their professions.

Accordingly, one of the first questions asked was, "Were you coerced into the industry?" Thirty-nine of the women (95%) said no; three of them were emphatic about the answer, including exclamation points. One woman did not give a yes or no response, but wrote instead "monetary problems." Another responded yes and explained: "A friend (female) persuaded me. She was working for a service. She introduced me. I could kill her now."

The survey followed up immediately with the question, "Do you know of women who were coerced?" Thirty-six women (88%) said no. Four women (10%) said yes. In describing the circumstances of the coercion they had heard of, three of the women reported: (1) "I am an outreach worker for street-walkers"; (2) "She had a pimp and he threatened her into it"; and, (3) "I have known many women in this field, but only one that was coerced. When she was twelve years old, her father put her on the street to supply his drug use."

In a separate interview with Norma Jean Almodovar, Executive Director of COYOTE, I asked her the same two questions. The lady adamantly replied no, then added how proud she was of having been a whore (her own word). Regarding other women who may have been coerced, Norma Jean—who personally knows hundreds of female sex workers—replied:

"I don't know of any women who have been coerced into the industry. Nor do I hear stories about coercion into prostitution or sex work. I only hear about coercion afterward by the police or by clients. I know it must exist. I know on the street level, it must exist."

Next, I asked the women surveyed to check off (from a prepared list) what they considered to be the main attractions of sex work. 95% cited money; 68%, sense of control; 54%, curiosity;

37%, rebellion; 15% acceptance. (Answers total more than 100% due to multiple responses.) Among the expanded answers written into the blank provided were:

—leisure
—meeting people and having nice things
—I can lay down, have fun, be looked at, have more fun, and be paid money
—learned to love the person in front of me; got over inhibitions, wanted to grow as a woman
—nonphysical work
—men treat me better when they pay me and the women I met could be trusted (a little) better
—for an attractive young woman with only a high school education, the opportunity for high financial gain and the chance to see the world first class on other people's money was extremely appealing. A woman in this business has to learn to negotiate for what *she* wants out of the encounter. She also has to ensure that she is treated with respect. Anything less is unacceptable.
—it became comfortable to me because of temporary relationships. Less complicated.

I asked what the main disadvantages of sex work were. 49% of the women cited social stigma; 41%, the police; 17%, the risk of physical harm; 15%, poor hours; 10%, unpleasant customers; 7%, no security; 7%, low self-esteem; 7%, can't have romantic relationship. (Answers total more than 100% due to multiple responses.) Among other answers written in were:

—It's a trap, Wendy, and I'm a smart woman so I know this.
—The money is the primary issue, because it is about

addiction (to money). Your perception about
things changes.

—I objectify men. They're only a means to an end.

—having sex with revolting men

—Having sex with men you aren't attracted to can be
boring, like any other job.

—no job future due to the aging factor

—It's often alienating and when I started the
business, many of the people I had to work with
were addicted to drugs.

A key question was, "Do you want to quit?" Eighteen women
(44%) said no; ten (24%) were not sure; seven (17%) said yes.
How long did they intend to remain in sex work? Ten women
(24%) said "as long as possible"; ten women didn't know. Of the
eight women (20%) who stated a definite time, both the median
and most common reply was two years; the range was a few
months to ten years.

The next major category of questions had to do with whether
the women had ever experienced violence as a result of sex work.
Twenty-nine women (71%) said no; twelve women (29%) said
yes. Norma Jean spoke to me of her own career as a call girl:

"I have never been a victim of violence since I have been a sex
worker. I do not consider myself unusual. If you are on the street
and you are dealing with someone who can remain anonymous, it
is more likely that people you will encounter will be violent.
Whereas women off the street are better able to get information
about their client and verify who he really is. This puts him in a
position of being identified and he is less likely to be violent. On
the street, there is a tremendous amount of violence toward the
women."

Of the twelve women who had experienced violence, nine of
them had been abused by a client, two of them by a boyfriend,
and one by a policeman.

As to how many of the women had dealt with the police, the sampling split down the middle. Twenty had; twenty hadn't; one was unclear. One prostitute was kind enough to answer my question at length:

"The other cost has been the police harassment. They can't bust me on prostitution so they try to on . . . felony fraud for baiting and misrepresenting my intentions." When a client pursued her and pulled out a gun, she ran to the police for protection. "The police asked my name and I was afraid the client would access my name and address from the police report. I begged the officer not to ask me because I was afraid of retaliation and he would not accept it, so I gave him a fake name. When he discovered it would not verify, he arrested me and I became hysterical. He then went on to charge me with disorderly conduct."

In expanding on their answers, the twenty women who had dealt with the police sometimes described them as "friends" or "clients." When I asked Norma Jean about this, she replied that vice cops are supposed to make arrests, but a lot of them "know that the women are not coerced into this business. They are not causing trouble . . . so they see an opportunity to use the woman's services—for free sometimes, sometimes more honestly."

The services the police use are not always sexual, as Norma Jean informed me: "Prostitutes make perfect stool pigeons because they are vulnerable and have always been a source of information for the police."

In approaching the issue of "economic coercion"—the common feminist claim that a need for money "forces" women into sex work—I asked a series of questions aimed at establishing what economic alternatives were available to the women and what rewards they received from sex work.

The "other" jobs that the women had held ranged from waitress, receptionist, and secretary to nurse, archaeologist, and TV news editor. In terms of education—often a good indicator of economic alternatives—thirty-seven (90%) of the women had finished high school. Twenty-one women (51%) had a college degree, while an additional seven (17%) had "some" college. Nineteen women (46%) were currently pursuing further education.

I asked the women to estimate how much they earned per week at previously held non-sex work jobs, and how much they earned per week as sex workers. Only twenty-nine women provided statistically useful information. Based on this data, the mean weekly income for previous non-sex work was $490; the mean weekly income for sex work was $2,360. The lowest paid form of sex work reported was "phone sex" ($40/hr.); the highest paid form of sex work reported was "call girl" ($100–$800/hr.).

I asked the women to estimate how many hours per week they had previously worked, and how many hours they worked now. Thirty-two women responded in a statistically useful manner. The mean number of hours per week for non-sex work came to forty-one. The mean number of hours per week for sex work came to nineteen.

To combine the above mean results: working a forty-one-hour week, women earned $490 at non-sex work. Working a nineteen-hour week, women earned $2,360 at sex work. For less than half the hours, they made close to five times the money.

I asked Norma Jean (formerly employed by the Los Angeles Police Department as a traffic officer) whether she had entered prostitution because she perceived no other economic alternative? She replied:

"No. I am an artist. I have been doing ceramic dolls for many, many years. The money I could make as a prostitute was significantly greater than as an artist. I could have earned a living, but could I have made that much money? Of course not."

The next category of questions was aimed at shedding light on the contention that women are driven into sex work due to traumas from their past—e.g., childhood sexual abuse. I asked the women to assess their childhoods as happy, average, or unhappy. (As a caveat: Most women I know, who are not sex workers, consider their childhoods to have been unhappy.) Seven women (17%) reported happy childhoods; twenty (49%) checked average; and nine (22%) said unhappy. Ten women (24%) said they had been sexually molested as children. Eight women (20%) reported having been physically molested—e.g., spankings or other forms of battery.

I asked a series of questions designed to ascertain whether the women—once they had entered sex work—felt free to enter the mainstream of society in other areas. I began with the query, "Are you engaged in charitable or community activities?" Twenty-two women (54%) replied yes. Eleven women (27%) were active in politics. Fifteen women (37%) attended church. In answer to the question, "Does sex work prevent involvement in the above?", twenty-two women (54%) replied no; ten (24%) said yes; and three (7%) answered "somewhat."

Next, I wanted to judge whether these sex workers had any interest in feminism. Twenty-five of the women (61%) had never attended a feminist meeting; sixteen of them (39%) had attended at least one meeting. In response to the question "Does modern feminism represent you?" fifteen women (37%) said yes, twelve women (29%) said no, ten women (24%) "didn't know," and four women (10%) felt "somewhat represented." The most common reason stated by those who felt represented was "because modern feminism is for equal rights between the sexes." The most common reason stated by those who felt unrepresented was "because modern feminism is anti sex workers."

Has becoming a sex worker changed the attitudes of the women toward themselves? Men? Other women? Sex in general? Since becoming sex workers, thirty-four women (83%) felt more comfortable/confident sexually; four women (10%) felt less confident. Thirty women (73%) experienced no change in their sexual orientation; five women (12%) altered their orientation, usually toward bisexualism.

Regarding attitudes toward men, twenty-nine women (71%)

reported a change; twelve women (29%) said none had occurred. Of the women whose attitudes had changed, typical comments in response to the question "How?" were:

—I'm more understanding about men's sexuality and what they want from women.
—I don't trust them as much. Think they mostly all cheat.
—I'm not afraid of them anymore.
—I'm not looking for my knight in a g-string with a great clean cock.
—I see them as more vulnerable.
—I realize that the majority of men are liars, pigs, and good for nothing.

Regarding attitudes toward other women, twenty-three women (56%) experienced no change; fifteen women (37%) did have a change of attitude. Of the latter group, eleven women reported that their attitudes toward women improved. The four with negative changes commented:

—Women who aren't sex workers are judgmental of sex workers.
—If they find out I work for an escort service, they begin to look at me differently, like dirt under their feet.
—Most women live in a fantasy, such as that their men don't cheat.
—A lot of women will do a lot of things for money.

In answer to the final question, "What is the single greatest misconception people have about sex work?" the most common answer—given by 16 women (39%)—was that prostitutes are bad people (e.g., sluts, uneducated, drug addicts). The second most common misconception, cited by nine women (22%), was that sex work was degrading.

A SAMPLE SURVEY OF COYOTE MEMBERS
This questionnaire was distributed to the membership of COY-OTE. The preceding survey results are based on the answers I received. The blank questionnaire is included to provide perspective on the survey and is not meant to be completed by readers.

My name is Wendy McElroy. I am currently working on a book defending the rights of sex workers. To do so effectively, the book must provide an accurate sense of women in the industry. To this end, Norma Jean Almodovar, Executive Director of COYOTE, has offered to forward this letter to you.

Please answer the following questions with as much or as little detail as you wish, using the back of pages to expand on answers. If any question seems intrusive, please skip it. A self-addressed stamped envelope is enclosed for your convenience in replying.

The survey is anonymous. If you wish to have me follow-up on your questionnaire (e.g., through a phone interview), please include your name and number. Otherwise, the line immediately following should be left blank.

Name & Number: _____

BACKGROUND IN SEX WORK
What type of sex work are you involved in? _____
At what age did you enter sex work? _____
How did you enter sex work? _____
Were you coerced into the industry? yes_____ no_____
    If yes, please describe _____
Do you know of women who were coerced? yes_____ no_____
    If so, please describe _____
The attractions of sex work are/were: money____curiosity____
    acceptance____ rebellion____ sense of control____ other____

The main attraction is/was _____
The disadvantages of sex work are _____
How long will you continue in sex work? _____
Do you want to quit? yes_____ no_____ not sure_____
As a sex worker, have you been a victim of violence? _____
    If yes, by whom (e.g., a client) _____
    Please describe circumstances _____
Have you dealt with the police? yes_____ no_____
    If yes, please describe _____

EMPLOYMENT BACKGROUND
What jobs have you held? _____
On average, how much were you paid? _____
How much are you paid now? _____
On average, how many hours did you work a week? _____
How many now? _____
What about your present working conditions would you
change? _____
What is your ideal job? _____

FAMILY BACKGROUND
Would you describe your childhood as:
    happy_____ average_____ unhappy_____ other _____
Were you sexually abused as a child? yes_____ no_____
Were you otherwise physically abused? yes_____ no_____
Do you have children? yes_____ no_____
Do family members know of your employment? yes____ no____
Are they supportive?
    Children _____
    Husband _____
    Parents _____

EDUCATIONAL BACKGROUND
Are you engaged in charitable or community activities? _____
    If so, please describe _____

Are you engaged in political activities? yes_____ no_____
    If so, please describe _____
Does being a sex worker keep you from involvement? _____
    If so, how? _____
Do you attend church? yes_____ no_____
Have you ever attended a feminist meeting? yes_____ no_____
Does modern feminism represent you? yes_____ no_____
    If yes, please explain _____
    If no, please explain _____

SEXUAL ATTITUDES

Since becoming a sex worker . . .
    I am more comfortable/confident sexually _____
    I am less comfortable/confident sexually _____
    My sexual orientation (gay/hetero) has changed _____
        If so how? _____
    My attitude toward men has changed: yes_____ no_____
        If yes, how? _____
    My attitude toward women has changed: yes_____ no_____
        If yes, how? _____
Please describe any other changes: _____
What is the single greatest misconception people have about sex
work? _____

CONCLUSION

The women who answered my survey ranged widely in age, educational background, and attitudes toward sex work. Some were
bitter and suspicious; they told me their friends had cautioned
them not to respond to my survey because it was obviously a
"police trap." Others seemed charmed by a "straight" woman
who wasn't passing judgment on them—who was purely and
simply curious. These women crammed information into the
small blanks of their surveys, then often attached sheet after sheet

of handwritten notes of further explanation.

I was bowled over by the honesty and intelligence of the responses I received. I was left to wonder whether if I were engaged in an illegal/semilegal activity, I would stand up and so expose myself.

END NOTES

CHAPTER ONE. PORNOGRAPHY AS AN INDUSTRY
1. Press Release from Ad Hoc Committee of Feminists for Free Expression (February 14, 1992).

CHAPTER TWO. DEFINING PORNOGRAPHY
1. *Jacobellis* v. *Ohio,* 378 U.S. 184, 197 (1964).
2. Andrea Dworkin, *Pornography: Men Possessing Women* (New York, NY: Penguin USA, 1989), p. 200.
3. D. H. Lawrence, *Pornography and Obscenity* (New York, NY: Knopf, 1930), pp. 1–2.
4. Catharine A. MacKinnon, *Only Words* (Cambridge, Mass.: Harvard University Press, 1993), p. 16.
5. *Only Words*, p. 3.
6. *Ms. Magazine*, January/February 1994, p. 34.
7. *Pornography: Men Possessing Women*, p. 13, 51, 53, 65.
8. The model anti-pornography ordinance can be found in Andrea Dworkin, "Against the Male Flood: Censorship, Pornography, and Equality," Harvard Women's Law Journal 8 (1985).

9. Jillian Ridington, *Confronting Pornography: A Feminist on the Front Lines* (Vancouver, Can.: CRIAW/ICREF, 1989), p. 27.

10. Joanna Russ, *Magic Mommas, Trembling Sisters, Puritans and Perverts* (Trumansburg, NY: The Crossing Press), p. 90.

CHAPTER THREE. FEMINISM AND PORN:
FELLOW TRAVELERS

1. Judith Walkowitz, *Prostitution and Victorian Society* (New York, NY: Cambridge University Press, 1980).

2. Yves Guyot, *English and French Morality from a Frenchman's Point of View* (London, England: 1885), p. 66.

3. *Prostitution and Victorian Society*, p. 248.

4. Act for the Suppression of Trade in and Circulation of, Obscene Literature and Articles of Immoral Use, (*Congressional Globe*, 1873), p. 297.

5. Abbie Kelly as quoted in Carrie Hapman Catt and Nettie Roger Shuler, *Woman Suffrage and Politics* (Seattle, Wash.: University of Washington Press, 1969), p. 37.

6. Sarah Grimke, *Letters on the Equality of the Sexes and the Condition of Woman* (New York, NY: Burt Franklin, 1837), Letter XII.

7. Linda Gordon, *Woman's Body, Woman's Right* (New York, NY: Penguin USA, 1976), pp. 117–118.

8. Angela Heywood in *The Word* (April, 1881). The Massachusetts State Historical Society has a full run on this periodical.

9. Anthony Comstock as quoted in Hal D. Sears *The Sex Radicals: Free Love in High Victorian America* (Lawrence, KS: Regents Press, 1977), p. 165.

10. *United States* v. *Bennett*, 24 Fed. Cas. (1879).

11. *Regina* v. *Hicklin*, England, L.R. 3 (1868).

12. Moses Harman, *Lucifer, the Light Bearer* (April 9, 1886).

13. The Kansas State Historical Society, Topeka, has a full run of *Lucifer*. The State Library in the State House, Topeka, has additional items on Harman.

14. *The New York Times*, (September 1, 1905), p. 1.
15. George Bernard Shaw in "Shaw v. America" in *London Opinion*, (January 30, 1909), p. 202.
16. Lizzie Holmes in *Lucifer* (August 28, 1891).
17. Lawrence Ladler, *The Margaret Sanger Story and the Fight for Birth Control* (Garden City, NY: Doubleday, 1955), p. 115.
18. *Butler* v. *Regina*, 1 S.C.R. (1992, Canada).
19. *Only Words*, p. 102.

CHAPTER FOUR. A CRITIQUE OF
ANTI-PORNOGRAPHY FEMINISM

1. *Regina* v. *Hicklin,* England, L.R. 3 (1868).
2. *Roth* v. *United States* 354 U.S. 976 (1957).
3. *Memoirs* v. *Massachusetts,* 383 U.S. 413 (1966).
4. *Roe* v. *Wade,* 410 U.S. 179 (1973).
5. *Miller* v. *California,* 413 U.S. 15, 34 (1973).
6. Susan Brownmiller, *Against Our Will* (New York, NY: Bantam, 1976), p. 5.
7. Catharine A. MacKinnon, *Toward A Feminist Theory of the State* (Cambridge, Mass.: Harvard, 1989).
8. *Only Words*, p. 28.
9. *American Booksellers Association, Inc.* v. *Hudnut*, 771 F. 2d. (1985).
10. *Barnes* v. *Glen Theatre*, Ill S.C. (1991).
11. *Butler* v. *Regina*, 1 S.C.R. (1992, Canada).
12. Press Release from Ad Hoc Committee of Feminists for Free Expression (February 14, 1992).
13. Dorchen Leidholdt and Janice G. Raymond, eds., *Sexual Liberals and the Attack on Feminism* (New York, NY: Pergamon Press, 1990), p. 136, 150, 157.
14. *The New York Times,* March 12, 1993, p. B16.
15. Nadine Strossen, *Virginia Law Review*, August 1993, p. 1183.

16. *Sourcebook on Pornography*, eds. Franklin Mark Osanka and Sara Lee Johann (Massachusetts: Lexington Books, 1989), p. 3.

17. President's Commission on Obscenity and Pornography, Report (New York, NY: Bantam, 1970), p. 243.

18. *United States of America* v. *Sex: How the Meese Commission Lied About Pornography* (New York, NY: Minotaur Press, 1986), p. 24.

CHAPTER FIVE. LIBERAL FEMINISM:
THE GLIMMER OF HOPE

1. *Virginia Law Review*, August 1993, p. 1118.

2. Indianapolis-Mercer Country; Indiana, General Ordinances Nos. 24 and 25 (1984), amendments to code of Indianapolis and Marion County.

3. *Schiro* v. *Clark*, 63 F.2d. 962, 972 (7th Cir. 1992).

4. Lisa Steel, "A Capital Idea," *Women Against Censorship* ed. Varda Burstyn (Vancouver, Can.: Douglas & McIntyre, 1985), p. 63.

5. Jill Ridington, as quoted in *Women Against Censorship*, p. 34.

CHAPTER SIX. INDIVIDUALIST FEMINISM:
A TRUE DEFENSE OF PORNOGRAPHY

1. Lillian Harman as quoted in Hal D. Sears, *The Sex Radicals*, p. 258.

2. *Harper's*, February, 1992, p. 42.

3. James R. Petersen, Forum, *Playboy*, March 1994.

4. *Perspectives on Pornography: Sexuality in Film and Literature*, eds. Gary Day and Clive Bloom (New York, NY: St. Martin's Press), p. 5.

5. *Magic Mommas . . .* , pp. 92–93.

6. *Freedom, Rights and Pornography: A Collection of Papers by Fred R. Berger*, ed. Bruce Russell (Boston, MA: Dordrecht Kluwer Academic Publishers, 1991), p. 138.

7. Janice A. Raymond, *Women as Wombs: Reproductive Tech-*

nologies and the Battle Over Women's Freedom (San Francisco, Calif.: Harper, 1993), p. 100.

8. *Magic Mommas . . .* , pp. 62–63.

9. Leonore Tiefer, "On Censorship and Women," *American Theatre*, January 1991, pp. 50–51.

10. Catharine MacKinnon admits that pornography will just be driven underground, *Feminism Unmodified* (Cambridge, MA: Harvard University Press, 1987), p. 146.

CHAPTER NINE. A COYOTE MEETING

1. *Vanity Fair*, February 1994.

2. *Los Angeles Times*, August 11, 1993.

INDEX